Praise for
9 of 1:
A Window to the World

"This is a very thoughtful book and an interesting approach to the subject of what brought us to the current world we live in and how different perspectives of the same events can change one's thoughts about it. The art work is well thought out, expertly laid out, and blends with large amounts of text or none at all as the story demands. We get the feel of the multi-cultural nature of our own country and the realization of how small the world has become. I am enthralled by what I have read.... Oliver succeeds by not making this a patriotic drum beating nor a propaganda piece for anti-war. It is an objective approach to a lot of components that make up an intricate mosaic. It is part history, part geography, part civics, and a lot of human relations. This is superb work."
— The Comic Book Network

"The series — which tells how nine students from a fictitious Fremont high school grapple with the events of Sept. 11 — serves as an alternative medium for airing viewpoints not represented by the mainstream media ... comics, especially in times of uncertainty, can serve as an important tool to send positive, educational messages."
— *The Argus*, Fremont, California

"[A] well-researched primer on different cultures and how several American students, of various nationalities, perceive these cultures and how they felt about 9/11 ... it's an educational tool ... an effective method for teachers to impart some current events knowledge, gauge student emotions and concerns, and perhaps generate compassion for people, cultures and ideologies they previously didn't understand. A worthy goal, and more power to him."
— moviepoopshoot

"The narration is a flowing entity, shifting from one voice to another to another, throughout the whole issue, and that unusual approach is reflected in the artwork and layout as well. In a way, it reminded me of the unconventional approach one finds in Scott McCloud's *Understanding Comics* and *Reinventing Comics*.... Expressing unpopular ideas and protesting against government were once symbols of what it is to be American, but now, those notions are considered by some who claim to be patriots as being wholly un-American and bordering on treason. Chin's work here offers a more balanced perspective.... Despite what [others] may have to say on the matter, books like *9 of 1* and other forms of balanced, intelligent examination of the after-effects of 9/11 are still to be found in America."
— TheFourthRail.com

9 of 1

A Window to the World

"A great nation receives all that flows into it."
— Lao Tzu, *Tao Te Ching*, Chapter 61

Oliver Chin

Frog, Ltd.
Berkeley, California

Published by Frog, Ltd.

Frog, Ltd. books are distributed by
North Atlantic Books
P.O. Box 12327
Berkeley, California 94712

ISBN 1-58394-043-X
Library of Congress Catalog Card number 2003006843

Cover and book design by Oliver Chin

Printed in the United States of America

North Atlantic Books' publications are available through most bookstores. For further information, call 800-337-2665 or visit our website at www.northatlanticbooks.com.

Substantial discounts on bulk quantities are available to corporations, professional associations, and other organizations. For details and discount information, contact our special sales department.

Library of Congress Cataloging-in-Publication Data

Chin, Oliver Clyde, 1969–
    Nine of one : a window to the world / by Oliver Chin. — 1st ed.
      p. cm.
Summary: Graphic novel in which nine members of an eleventh grade United States History class present oral reports on the reactions of diverse strangers to the terrorist attacks of September 11, 2001.
    ISBN 1-58394-072-3
    [1. September 11 Terrorist Attacks, 2001 — Fiction. 2. World politics — 1995–2005 — Fiction. 3. Homework — Fiction. 4. Schools — Fiction.] I. Title.
    PZ7.C44235Ni 2003
    [Fic] — dc21
                              2003006843

1 2 3 4 5 6 7 8 9 DATA 08 07 06 05 04 03

Contents

To my father and mother,
Henry and Naida,
for bringing me into the world
and putting their world in me.

oreword

When Oliver asked me to write this introduction, I said "Yes" without really meaning it, which is the predictable response of insecure, love-starved people like me, who are surprised when they're wanted by anyone for whatever reason.

However, when I finally received the manuscript and reluctantly opened it and sat down to read it, my guilt and dread for having agreed to something that required me to be responsible was gradually transformed to enthusiasm. The book was engaging and entertaining and instructive and brought me back face to face with the richness of the East Bay, my former home.

The story develops as a group of high school students in Fremont, California, struggles to gain insight into the events of September 11 and what they mean both personally and politically. They interview neighbors, distant relatives, friends of friends, ultimately learning about their own place in a fractured and fractious world. There are no pat answers, no central dogma; instead, each student struggles to understand and respond to the calamitous events in the context of their own unique culture and background.

Through these students, Oliver thoughtfully traces threads of social and political meaning, bringing the shock and horror of September 11 into a tragic but comprehensible manifestation of a world in disarray. His drawings help the reader span the world, and make real and immediate the distant cultures and disparate players in these heady events.

This is a unique book, one that will speak directly to any teenager — indeed anyone of any age — interested in seeing the world as it is, the better to find ways to improve it. We are led to face unhappy truths about the world, but always with an underlying sense of hope and optimism.

Oliver has crafted a deeply felt, honest rumination on what it is like to be a teen in these strange times, and one that is surprisingly free of the easy cynicism that is the instinctive response of youth to the insolence and hypocrisy of the powers that be. He lets young people (and older people as well) speak for themselves, showing us an America that is full of heart, that is robust and vigorous, and this dynamism clearly springs from the rich diversity of people and opinions that he finds here. It is marvelous that he has captured this spirit at this critical time.

— Phoebe A.G.S. Gloeckner

rologue

"One day posterity will remember this strange era,
these strange times,
when ordinary
common honesty was called courage."
— Yevgeny Yevtushenko, Russian poet

oday current events have managed to outpace people's wildest imagina-
tions and their very ability to keep up with the news. "The new electronic
independence re-creates the world in the image of a global village," wrote
Canadian writer Marshall McLuhan in his 1968 book *War and Peace in the Global
Village*. Truly, before our very eyes, we have seen our world grow smaller by the
day but yet more divided.

In what seems an endless parade, an array of
pressures throughout states, nations, and conti-
nents continues to pit one culture's beliefs and
resources against another's. These pressures are
political and social, economic and environmental,
historic and militaristic, ideological and religious.
Therefore, the challenge is greater than ever to
form opinions on what one hears, reads, and sees.

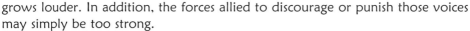

But wherever these struggles take place, words
tend to get drowned out as the clamor for deeds
grows louder. In addition, the forces allied to discourage or punish those voices
may simply be too strong.

Yet, together we have entered the 21st century facing enormous and manifold
problems that require not only respectful debate but also mutual cooperation to
solve. With that in mind, ideas really do matter. Indeed, one person's conviction
can make a difference. And preserving a democracy, based upon the right of
individuals to exercise free speech and act upon those convictions responsibly in
concert with others, has never been more important.

Everybody has something to say. But sometimes you can find out what that is only
when you ask them.

- -

This story follows nine California teenagers who try to make sense of the tumult
following one international crisis. The students from James Madison High School

are chomping on the bit of adulthood. But in the wake of September 11th, they confront the words and deeds of adults who have tipped their world off its axis.

As people around the globe grapple with the aftershocks of this catastrophe, an 11th-grade history teacher challenges his students to move forward: can they become reporters and seek answers within a jumble of emotions, facts, and points of view?

With open minds and sharpened pencils, these teens scratch through the surface of misunderstanding to find that this story is not simple or uniform. Are black and white, good and evil, and right and wrong not merely in the eye of the beholder, but also in the voice of the narrator?

Fanning out to interview strangers within their midst, these youth field a spectrum of opinions from a multicultural community both native and foreign to their ears: Afghani and Soviet, Arab and Jew, Asian and Indian, and Latino and Black.

Listening to tales from around the world, these students discover that we have to learn from history to not repeat it.

Introduction

They call this place "Little Kabul."

It was named in homage to the capital of their homeland, a domain that spawned generations of legendary Khans along with those of nameless herdsmen.

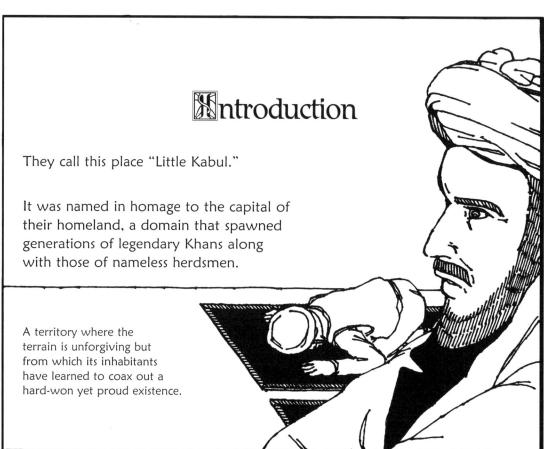

A territory where the terrain is unforgiving but from which its inhabitants have learned to coax out a hard-won yet proud existence.

Now in this place a thriving bazaar has been formed by the many tribes of a diaspora.

Afghan brothers
reuniting again.

Ethnic Pashtuns
holding court.

Devout Shiites
teaching their faith.

This place quickly became a vibrant locus for a community searching for a new home.
For those travelers to barter goods and stories. For those refugees seeking solace from the
unforgettable and unbearable memories of all-too-familiar conflict.

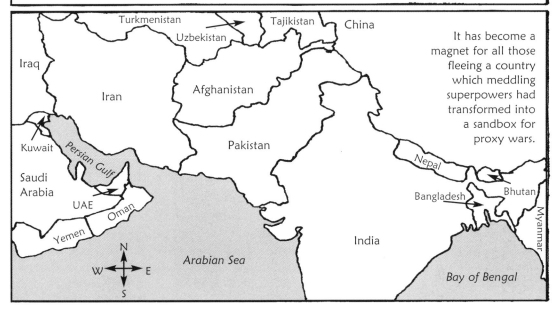

It has become a magnet for all those fleeing a country which meddling superpowers had transformed into a sandbox for proxy wars.

A succession of foreign invaders had come just in the last century alone.

The British.   The Russians.   The Americans.

Now situated in this town, uneasily eyed by the natives, people start over again.

While trying to regain a semblance of normalcy,

recent arrivals confront a new way of life, where their rituals and traditions face the unknown.

Where the past ...

its history and its horrors, must be woven together with the dreams of a better future.

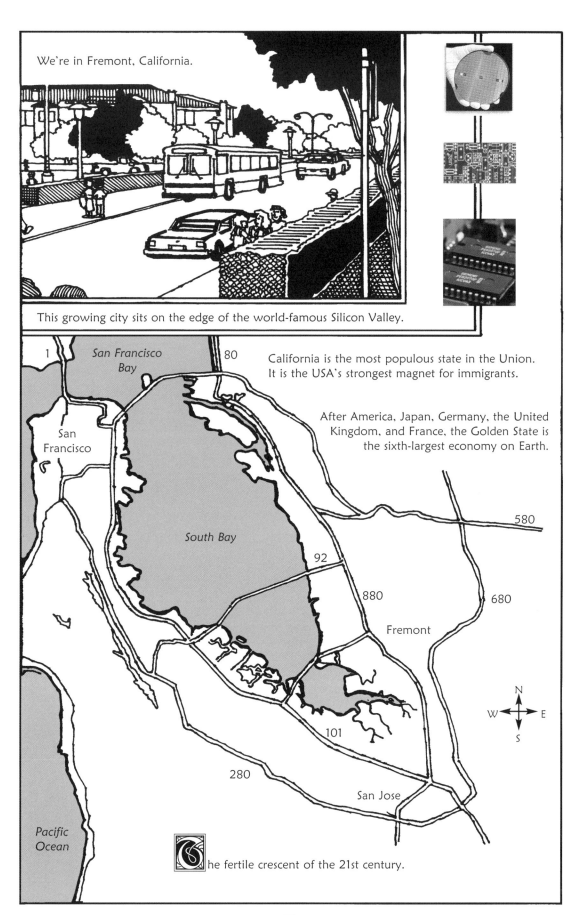

We're in Fremont, California.

This growing city sits on the edge of the world-famous Silicon Valley.

California is the most populous state in the Union. It is the USA's strongest magnet for immigrants.

After America, Japan, Germany, the United Kingdom, and France, the Golden State is the sixth-largest economy on Earth.

San Francisco Bay

San Francisco

South Bay

Fremont

San Jose

Pacific Ocean

The fertile crescent of the 21st century.

"Learning is ever in the freshness of its youth, even for the old."
— Aeschylus (525–456 B.C.)

In nearby Union City the 2001 school year had started simply enough. In most of California, autumn hardly seems to be a distinct season.

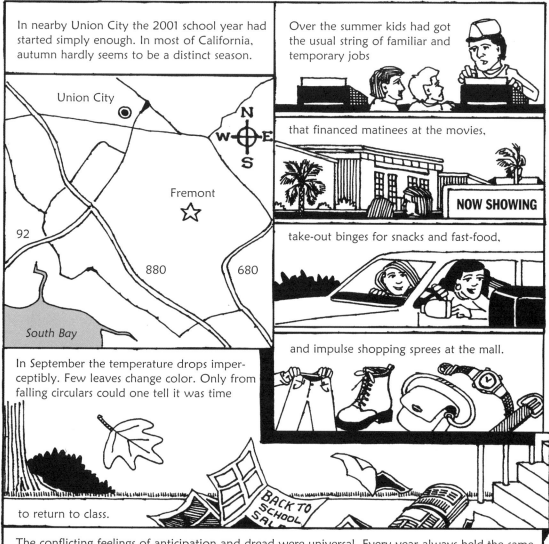

Over the summer kids had got the usual string of familiar and temporary jobs

that financed matinees at the movies,

NOW SHOWING

take-out binges for snacks and fast-food,

and impulse shopping sprees at the mall.

In September the temperature drops imperceptibly. Few leaves change color. Only from falling circulars could one tell it was time

BACK TO SCHOOL SALE

to return to class.

The conflicting feelings of anticipation and dread were universal. Every year always held the same challenges, no matter what one's age. Forging friendships through trial and error. Acting as cool as allowable. Jockeying for grades. Fitting in with social cliques. Satisfying parents and teachers while trying to find your own way in your own style and pace. No one ever said it was easy.

September 10th seemed just like every other day. Normal. Plain. Uneventful.

Julie Lai

"I don't recall too much about it, really.

I think it was a sunny day. Not a bad way to start a Monday morning.

For me, it was just the start of yet another long week before we could enjoy the weekend."

Others remembered their ordinary habits.

"My mom dropped me off at the front of school as usual.

I kissed her on the cheek and then said goodbye.

Raman Patel

I remember that I had decided to break in a new pair of shoes that my parents had given me for my birthday."

On September 11th, 2001, that all changed.

James Madison High School, 8:00 A.M.

Soon people were starting to talk all about it.

"I hadn't heard the news before I left for school. But as soon as I got there, I did.

I didn't expect anything special to happen that day. Really, at first I didn't know what was going on. The next thing I knew, my friends and I were trying to listen to the radio or make a phone call home. But some kids still weren't taking it too seriously."

Valerie Silverberg

"Rumors were spreading fast.

Homeroom was quickly getting out of control. It was like being in a fire drill but we didn't know where to go or what to do.

Everyone suddenly started feeling the same thing. It wasn't panic, just a lingering sense of disbelief and then dismay. Of course none of us could really believe all the reports, until we finally saw the footage with our own eyes."

Celeste Quincy

"It was worse than any stupid movie."

Hector Gonzalez

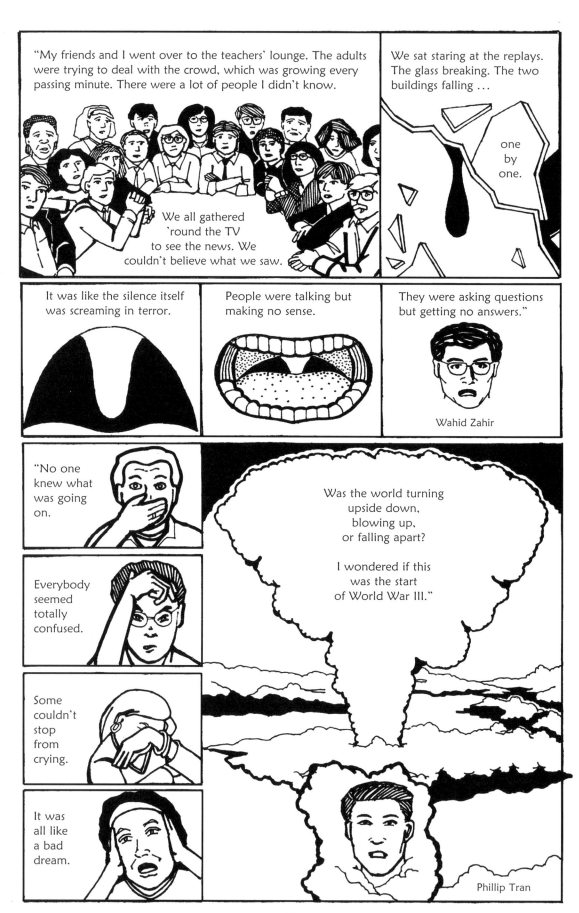

"My friends and I went over to the teachers' lounge. The adults were trying to deal with the crowd, which was growing every passing minute. There were a lot of people I didn't know.

We all gathered 'round the TV to see the news. We couldn't believe what we saw.

We sat staring at the replays. The glass breaking. The two buildings falling ...

one by one.

It was like the silence itself was screaming in terror.

People were talking but making no sense.

They were asking questions but getting no answers."

Wahid Zahir

"No one knew what was going on.

Everybody seemed totally confused.

Some couldn't stop from crying.

It was all like a bad dream.

Was the world turning upside down, blowing up, or falling apart?

I wondered if this was the start of World War III."

Phillip Tran

"The morning after, I didn't want to get out of bed.

I tried to wash the terrible taste of yesterday out of my mouth.

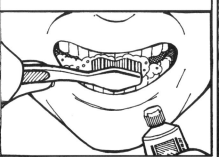

Some kids stayed home to watch TV.

We anxiously waited to be told what had just happened and why, but got hearsay mixed with slivers of facts instead.

ATTACK on AMERICA

They were clueless."

Xavier Frazier

"School feels like daycare. It's a place meant to keep us out of trouble.

Maylene Abellar

But often it feels more like a prison than it should.

Students have to undergo random drug testing.

Every single day, kids get frisked by security guards and metal detectors. It didn't feel right, going back there after what had just happened.

But that's where our friends were. Each one of us knew we needed someone to lean on. And that our friends needed to lean on us too."

After 9/11, students and teachers were both uncertain as to what to do.

"11th-grade U.S. history is hard to teach under normal circumstances. Now it suddenly felt impossible. I decided to ditch my lesson plan. I had no choice.

My whole class was distracted. Somehow I had to reengage my kids and make history relevant to what they were experiencing. But how?

We all wanted to understand these events but didn't know what the first step was. For the first time in their lives, America was attacked.

School officials and volunteers were scrambling to react. They were like bees swarming after a stick is shoved into their hive. It was chaos. In fact it wasn't much different from what we were reading in the daily newspapers or seeing on television.

Matthew Pearson
Teacher, James Madison

Realizing that they hadn't paid proper attention to the rest of the world, the media and politicians were both groping for answers.

There wasn't a better time to experiment. We really had nothing to lose.

Our government's actions inevitably were going to have global consequences. Seventeen-year-olds can't vote. But they can enlist and they can be drafted.

Diplomats from around the world already felt that the situation soon would be beyond their control.

If that was the case, how were my students supposed to feel?

So I decided to give my class a new assignment."

OM 222

OK, boys and girls, it's time to settle down.

Alright, everybody listen up now.

I'm changing our schedule and handing out a new project. We won't be following the textbook for the time being. Now I want each of you to give an oral report. It's going to be due at the end of the semester.

Your goal is to interview a complete stranger, someone you've never met before. He or she must be at least twice as old as you. I want you to ask them their opinions of the event that people are now calling "9/11."

How are we supposed to find a person we don't know?

Michelle, have you heard of the term "six degrees of separation"? It's a 20th-century theory that you can be connected to anyone else on the Earth by linking the acquaintances of five other people between you and them. They even made a play and a movie about this idea. In our case, I want each of you to ask someone to introduce you to a person who has a totally different background from your own. It may take some time, but I know all of you can do it.

So it's like I know Kobe Bryant because my dad has a friend whose son went to school with him? Is that right?

Yep, that's the idea. I want you to ask your "stranger" what they think about what just happened. How they see the world may be totally different from how you do. But remember, prejudice mean "pre-judging." It is the mistake of assuming you know all the angles when you don't. You may disagree with them, but it's your job to let them say their piece. Then you can evaluate where they're coming from and why.

Boy, that's really stretching it, John.

History is not just about gathering facts. It's also about how we interpret them.

Well, after that class the planet kept spinning. Initially, we didn't know what to make of Mr. Pearson's assignment. Some thought it was off the wall. Others took it to be a vacation since we didn't have nightly reading or homework. So we eased back into our normal routines.

Submerging ourselves in the familiar clubs and sports. The usual activities to pass the time.

Kicking back.

Socializing and hanging.

But life wasn't quite the same anymore. Little things, things we once ignored, now gave off unfamiliar and uncomfortable vibes.

Meanwhile the story kept growing more complicated, messy, and disturbing. Facts were hidden, twisted, and colored by opinions.

Then Mr. Pearson said each of us, even those students on the school paper, had to learn how to become media critics. What was that?

History became a journalism course. As readers and viewers, we consumed the news but didn't realize it. In print and on the radio. On TV and over the Web. Now we analyzed what was covered, and studied how and by whom. We learned to second-guess why certain stories were covered and others weren't.

Next we became novice producers of the news. We had to learn the tools of the trade. For example, we practiced how to frame a question and record the answers. We researched how to cite sources and the ways to put stories into context. To make it real, Mr. Pearson booked field trips to local newsrooms for us to observe reporters in action. We quizzed them on how they gathered information from primary and secondary sources and balanced differing points of view.

For some of them, the job was still a passion. For others, it had boiled down to being a business, driven by circulation and measured by revenue and profits.

In the beginning, it was totally cool if we weren't particularly great writers, speakers, or artists. At the start, journalism was trial and error for us. None of our first drafts were ever perfect. But with practice and training, we could improve our techniques, develop our styles, and hone our instincts. We learned how to ask the right questions, record the answers, and tell a story in a meaningful way.

So twenty-seven kids had a deadline to beat.

We asked our family for recommendations.

We hit the phones and started dialing ...

Friends for names of their friends ...

Gradually we chatted with a lot of different folks.

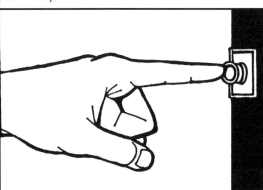

Eventually, everybody found a person to talk to. It's funny. Once they agreed to speak to us, they couldn't be strangers anymore. That's just the way life is.

As the semester drew to a close, we gathered back together to compare notes and conclusions. Each of us completed the task with varying degrees of success, as we recorded a spectrum of conflicting views. Mr. Pearson advised us to present them straight up but put their words in perspective. Listening to our classmates speak, we heard voices we didn't expect to hear. Each had its own tone and temperament. They surprised us. They provoked us. They taught us. Here are nine of their stories.

11th Grade History — Mr. Pearson: Class Report
Name: Maylene Abellar
Born: San Jose, California, 1985

I'm Filipino and Manuela, my older sister, was born in Manila. In 1984 my relatives finally succeeded in persuading my parents to come to the U.S. Even though I was born here, I speak Spanish and Tagalog, our native language.

Though it didn't hit me at the start, I realize that modern Filipino history is relevant to our project. America has had a big presence in the Philippines, but it wasn't always that way. Only a century ago, America became involved with the islands, which at that time were the spoils of another war.

After winning the Spanish American War, in 1898 the U.S. signed a peace treaty in which Spain agreed to hand over its colonies of Cuba, Puerto Rico, and the Philippines. In exchange for the Philippines, the U.S. specifically paid Spain twenty million dollars, and allowed Spain to continue their maritime trade for another decade. However, many Filipinos, who had fought the Spanish occupation, vowed to continue their armed struggle against any new foreign master.

At first, America occupied only the Philippines' capital of Manila. Lacking the popular support at home to forcibly annex all the country, President William McKinley was unsure of what to do. But one night while he slept, he said he heard the "voice of God." McKinley was told there was "nothing left for us to do but to take them all, to educate the Filipinos, and uplift and Christianize them."

Acting upon the president's divine inspiration, the U.S. quickly fanned a revolt into a civil war. Soon America stopped relying on a volunteer army and drafted 100,000 soldiers to defeat the island's rebels. However, the U.S. called the war an "insurrection" to minimize political dissent, as well as to avoid paying troops combat pay and benefits.

Mom and Dad, as newlyweds in Manila.

In 1902 President Theodore Roosevelt declared that hostilities had stopped, even though guerilla battles continued for another five years. In the end, the U.S. suffered about 7,000 casualties. However, historians estimate that native tribes lost over 500,000, the vast majority of whom were civilians.

Ironically, my grand uncle was part of the Filipino resistance that helped the U.S. Army expel the Japanese invaders in World War II. Later he came to live in San Francisco with many of his friends. But to this day, all of them have been denied any military benefits for their armed service, simply because they are not American citizens. Many Filipino WWII veterans continue to die on American soil, without having enough money to pay for their own funerals.

The U.S. still has a presence in the Philippines. Now "military advisors" are training the Filipino army to fight the Abu Sayyaf, one of the smallest and most radical Islamic groups, which wants to create an independent state. Arabic for "father of the swordsman," it is the name of a mujahedin fighter in the 1980s, with whom Filipino Muslims battled the Soviet-backed regime in Afghanistan.

Richard Denton works with my mom at an insurance company.

We had lunch together in Walnut Creek, near their office.

How did this event affect you personally?

I had a friend who worked at the World Trade Center.

He was missing for about two weeks before rescue teams found and identified a part of his body.

We met each other the first week of our freshman year in college. His name was Paul Antonelli. We shared the same dorm, a lotta all-nighters, and some pretty amazing times together. But I never admitted to him that he was a better basketball player than me.

It turns out that we were both from Philadelphia but we didn't know each other growing up. I'm Irish. He was Italian.

Now here we were best buddies. Living it up. Looking at big business careers ahead of us.

A century earlier, we would have been fighting each other on opposite sides of the street.

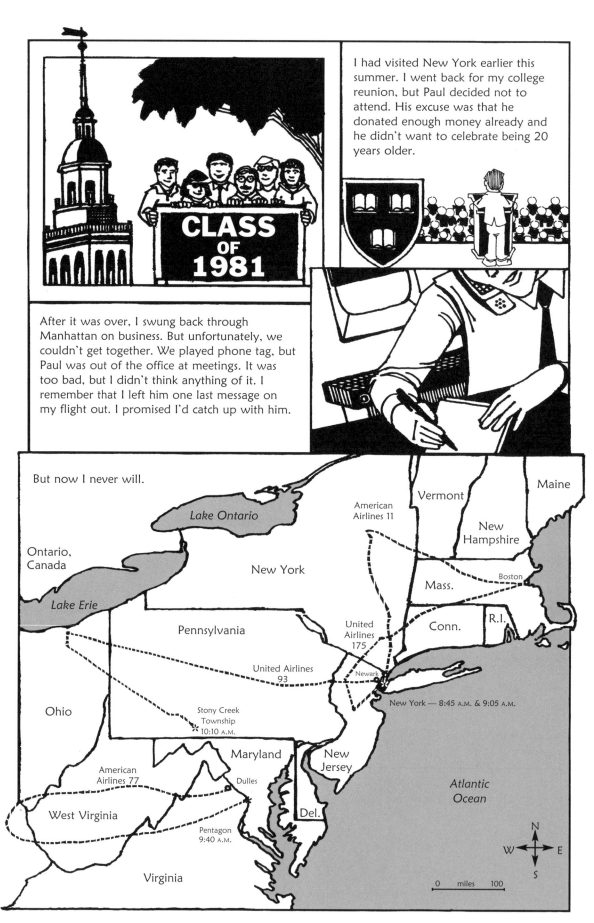

I had visited New York earlier this summer. I went back for my college reunion, but Paul decided not to attend. His excuse was that he donated enough money already and he didn't want to celebrate being 20 years older.

CLASS OF 1981

After it was over, I swung back through Manhattan on business. But unfortunately, we couldn't get together. We played phone tag, but Paul was out of the office at meetings. It was too bad, but I didn't think anything of it. I remember that I left him one last message on my flight out. I promised I'd catch up with him.

But now I never will.

Lake Ontario

Ontario, Canada

Lake Erie

New York

American Airlines 11

Vermont

Maine

New Hampshire

Mass.

Boston

Pennsylvania

United Airlines 175

Conn.

R.I.

United Airlines 93

Newark

Ohio

Stony Creek Township 10:10 A.M.

New York — 8:45 A.M. & 9:05 A.M.

Maryland

New Jersey

Atlantic Ocean

American Airlines 77

Dulles

Del.

West Virginia

Pentagon 9:40 A.M.

Virginia

N
W E
S

0 miles 100

Maylene: How did you feel when you heard about the crashes?

Richard: I felt confused and helpless. What did Paul ever do to them?

What did any of them do? Nothing at all.

It was like attacking the UN. There were people from every country on Earth. From dishwashers to stockbrokers. Hitting the Pentagon? That took balls.

Maylene: What do you miss about your friend?

Richard: I never pictured Paul as a soccer dad. But Paul said he enjoyed seeing his son play more than playing himself. I'll miss that type of generosity.

Paul left a wife and two kids. His wife Wendy is a trooper but I'm sure it will be hard on her. I don't know what his son Josh is going to do without him. Stephanie is almost ready to apply to college herself, just like you.

Maylene: What should America do now?

Richard: We need to find whoever did this and get them. The U.S. is the last superpower left. If we don't make these bastards pay, who will?

The world has to see them get punished.

The U.S. didn't ask to be the world's policeman. But we have to defend freedom, democracy, and the American way of life. If that means having to fight and die for it, by God, that's what we have to do.

We as Americans may have to make a few sacrifices here and there. I don't know what price we'll have to pay. But we have to make these terrorists sorry they ever thought about doing this to us. We can't let this type of thing happen again.

I don't say this lightly. My dad was a Marine who fought in the Korean War. He spoke of buddies who never came back. Back then President Eisenhower inherited the war and ended it. No stranger to blood-shed, the general had been the Allied supreme commander against Hitler. On the eve of another war, this time in southeast Asia, he warned of the dangers of the growing "military-industrial complex."

[Maylene: On January 17, 1961, President Dwight D. Eisenhower gave his farewell address to the nation. Here is an excerpt of the speech.] "A vital element in keeping the peace is our military establishment. Our arms must be mighty, ready for instant action, so that no potential aggressor may be tempted to risk his own destruction. Our military organization today bears little relation to that known by any of my predecessors in peacetime, or indeed by the fighting men of World War II or Korea.

Until the latest of our world conflicts, the United States had no armaments industry. American makers of plowshares could, with time and as required, make swords as well. But now we can no longer risk emergency improvisation of national defense; we have been compelled to create a permanent armaments industry of vast proportions. Added to this, three and a half million men and women are directly engaged in the defense establishment. We annually spend on military security more than the net income of all United States corporations.

This conjunction of an immense military establishment and a large arms industry is new in the American experience. The total influence — economic, political, even spiritual – is felt in every city, every Statehouse, every office of the Federal government. We recognize the imperative need for this development. Yet we must not fail to comprehend its grave implications. Our toil, resources and livelihood are all involved; so is the very structure of our society.

In the councils of government, we must guard against the acquisition of unwarranted influence, whether sought or unsought, by the military-industrial complex. The potential for the disastrous rise of misplaced power exists and will persist.

We must never let the weight of this combination endanger our liberties or democratic processes. We should take nothing for granted. Only an alert and knowledgeable citizenry can compel the proper meshing of the huge industrial and military machinery of defense with our peaceful methods and goals, so that security and liberty may prosper together."

Richard: But still, didn't our military and industries make America the most powerful nation on Earth?

Maylene: I've never been to New York. What was it like there before 9/11?

Richard: Those buildings were huge. You'd hurt your neck looking at them. Each tower was five times taller than anything we have out here. Then multiply that by two.

Manhattan is a crazy, manic, but often magical place. Everybody wants to make things happen.

People out here don't realize how big those towers were.

They rose like twin mountain peaks.

NO TURNS

YIELD

ONE WAY

WALK TO NEXT SIGN

NO PARKING ANYTIME

The noise and traffic can certainly get over-whelming. It's easy to get confused and lose your way. But the city pulses with life all the time. Day or night, it is a non-stop swarm of activity.

Fleets of taxis. A maze of metro subway lines. Waves of pedestrians in a hurry. The pace there is so fast, where every second seems to count.

Flying into the city, I instantly recognized the skyline. The towers were anchors. Shiny beacons. Compasses you always could count on.

Maylene: What do you think is going to happen next?

Richard: Who knows? That's the real problem. Suddenly, no one thinks they're safe, even if they're tucked away in the suburbs a thousand miles from the city. If something like that could happen there, then it could happen anywhere.

Do you have any final thoughts?

It's a weird, mixed-up feeling. Anger. Fear. Emptiness.

I can't help thinking about it, even when I don't want to. It's like I'm stuck on a merry-go-round in a nightmare. I don't know where to start or how to stop. The whole ordeal has been awful on Paul's family. It could have just as easily been me.

The last time I got to see Paul was when they laid him to rest.

I try to remember the good times we had. The qualities that made him a special friend.

At work I catch myself daydreaming about life ... its meaning.

I ask God why this had to happen, and I'm waiting for the answer.

11th Grade History — Mr. Pearson: Class Report
Name: Celeste Quincy
Born: London, England, 1985

I came to the States when I was ten. My dad works at a computer company, and he decided to transfer from the office in the United Kingdom to the headquarters here in Sunnyvale. I'm an only child, so it's just been us two. My mum died when I was nine. A drunk driver hit her car when she was coming home from work. Back then, I didn't understand why we had to leave so soon afterwards, but now I think my dad wanted a fresh start. I don't miss England that much anymore, though I do miss seeing my grandparents. But as my dad says, "We're in this together," so life has been ok.

Even though I haven't been here that long, people treat me like I'm an American. I take it as a compliment but I don't feel I've changed that much, really. Except that I'm gradually losing my English accent, which makes my pop a wee bit sad. He said that once that goes, he won't be able to tell the difference between a Californian and me.

California is almost twice as large as the English isles. Also, there's a lot of mixing of nationalities here. You see more types of restaurants on the street, food from places I might never go to in my lifetime. At school, students come from a wider range of cultures. We have clubs for pretty much everything you could think of: Blacks, Vietnamese, Chicanos, Indians (Eastern and American), Afghans, Muslims, and even one for Celts.

In general, the British tend to take a dim view of the Yanks. Back in the 1800s, the British Empire dominated the world, so I suppose it was hard to see the U.S. take our place in the 20th century. However, jealousy isn't the main reason. The English believe that Americans fit their stereotype of being outspoken and aggressive. That can rub the wrong way, when Americans ignore the opinions of others. In Europe, countries disagree but are more sensitive to what their neighbors think because everyone is so close together and has so much history to contend with.

My favoite sport is tennis. I'm on the JV team.

For my interview, I spoke with Usha Pasdar, who is the aunt of one of my friends at James Madison. Meena had told me that she admired her aunt a lot for being independent. She's like a role model, helping to organize women to get equal rights and treatment back in Afghanistan. It's impossible to change a rigid culture overnight.

Before we met, I did some research on Central Asia and was surprised by what I read. Formerly republics of the Soviet Union, Azerbaijan, Kazakhstan, Turkmenistan, and Uzbekistan discovered that they had trillions of dollars' worth of untapped oil and natural gas reserves. Because Afghanistan lies between these fields and the world's markets, the California oil corporation Unocal paid the Taliban for the rights to build and control a $2 billion pipeline in 1996. Unocal even hosted Talibs in its Texas offices, while the U.S. State Department denounced the Taliban's human rights record.

In 1998, Vice President Dick Cheney, then CEO of the gas company Halliburton, said, "The good Lord didn't see fit to put oil and gas only where there are democratically elected regimes friendly to the United States. Occasionally we have to operate in places where, all things considered, one would not normally choose to go. But, we go where the business is." The U.S. had pledged over $100 million and funded Pakistan's Inter-Services Intelligence to support the Afghan government ... all by May 2001.

Though I have known Meena for many years, I didn't get to meet other members of her family until fairly recently. To me, her family is like her house. Outside it looks like every other one on the block. But the inside is totally different. It is a blend of two worlds. For example, her cousin Rafi is a policeman. He's been on the force for four years. But five times a day, no matter where he is, Rafi points his mat toward Mecca and prays.

Meena's aunt Usha invited me to her office. When I arrived, she showed me the way into one of their large conference rooms that she had reserved for the interview. There we sat down in the plush leather recliners.

Then Usha began to tell me about her life...

Life is definitely different in America. Here everything is just a lot bigger. Houses. Cars. Even people. Everyone has a lot more room to live and move around. Cities are spread out and have no boundaries. Highways go on forever and gas is so cheap. Food is plentiful and never a concern.

Back in Afghanistan, I grew up in a small house made of adobe, brick, and dirt. The house had no indoor plumbing. We all used an outhouse in the backyard.

For generations my family learned to make do. But when I was about your age, I began to yearn for something more.

There comes a point where you have to stand up for your hopes and your beliefs. But people do need certain liberties to enjoy that privilege. These freedoms exist here but may just be a dream elsewhere.

Each morning here seems like a fresh start.

However, every day our community remembers loved ones who have been left behind or those still suffering. Also we mourn those who've perished.

Our past is not that far behind us. There, life has always been a challenge. The weather has never been kind. Nevertheless, against all reason and prayers, circumstances have continued to worsen throughout decades of war.

Countless bullets and bombs from untold raids, factions, and alliances have pulverized a once proud and vibrant civilization. Anarchy and random violence have become accepted parts of life. Poverty and deprivation are the rule.

Their towns erased, villagers are uprooted across borders to swelling refugee camps.

Left with no past and no future.

Clans are mired in endless cycles of retribution. Families bereft of fathers, husbands, and sons.

The Taliban flourished amid a civil war ...

... that followed the recent flight of the *Soviets* and the quick demise of their puppet government.

In this power vacuum, warlords, once united against a common enemy, turned on each other in a free-for-all. The populace was exhausted by war and naturally preferred a promise of order to the continued chaos.

Therefore Muslim mercenaries and religious fundamentalists coalesced behind the Taliban's emerging leadership.

Bamiyan Buddha, created 200–500 A.D.

However, the Taliban's ideology could brook no competition.

Unfortunately, soon the Taliban grew to be as repressive as the regime they replaced.

March 11, 2001

The new rulers brutally applied the lessons of survival that they had learned and their society had grown to rely upon.

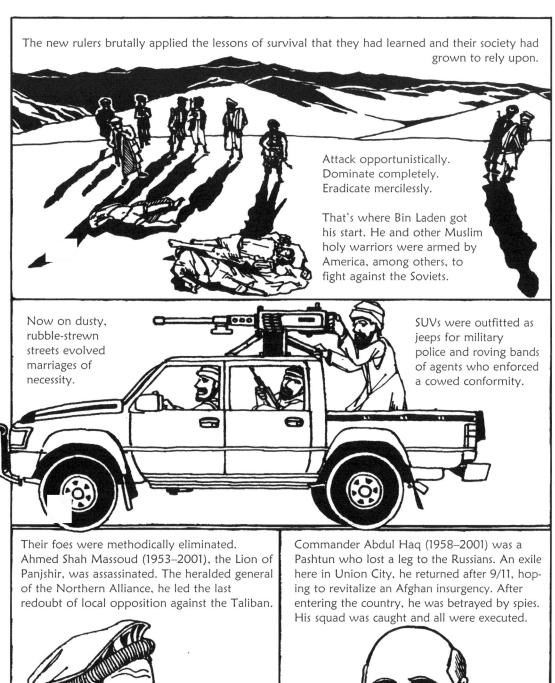

Attack opportunistically. Dominate completely. Eradicate mercilessly.

That's where Bin Laden got his start. He and other Muslim holy warriors were armed by America, among others, to fight against the Soviets.

Now on dusty, rubble-strewn streets evolved marriages of necessity.

SUVs were outfitted as jeeps for military police and roving bands of agents who enforced a cowed conformity.

Their foes were methodically eliminated. Ahmed Shah Massoud (1953–2001), the Lion of Panjshir, was assassinated. The heralded general of the Northern Alliance, he led the last redoubt of local opposition against the Taliban.

Commander Abdul Haq (1958–2001) was a Pashtun who lost a leg to the Russians. An exile here in Union City, he returned after 9/11, hoping to revitalize an Afghan insurgency. After entering the country, he was betrayed by spies. His squad was caught and all were executed.

He was murdered by two suicide bombers who were posing as journalists.

Now Haq's teenage son must assume his fallen mantle.

The Taliban's strict interpretation of the Koran dictated the proper role of women. Women wore the burqa as a symbol...

To hide emotion.

To cover the flesh.

To block the evils of temptation.

as submissive servants who knew to keep their proper place in their society.

The Taliban clerics exercised their authority with impunity.
In stadiums, playing soccer was banned.
In this sport's place were held public executions, which were grisly examples of how deviation would not be tolerated.

In accordance with upholding the "shariah code," all Western influences were deemed morally corrosive. Therefore music and television were outlawed too.

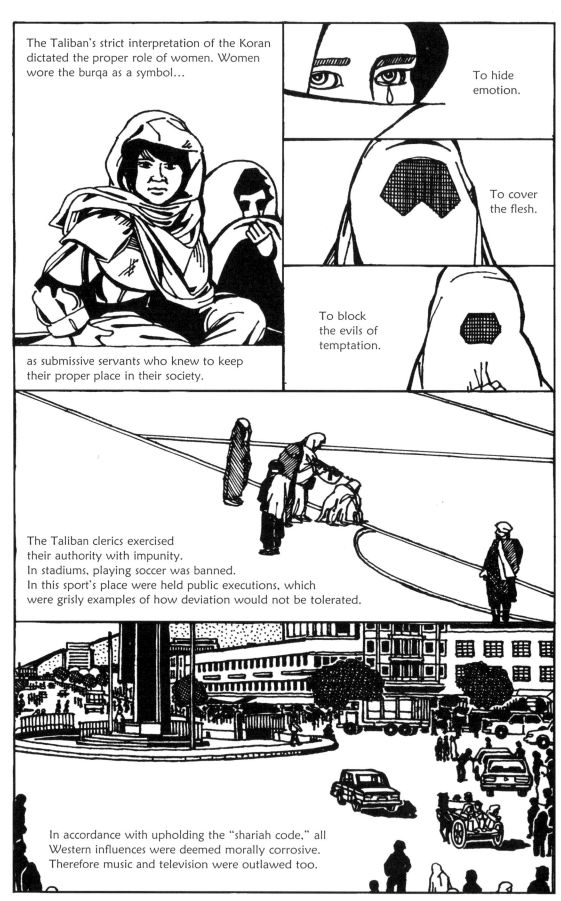

Now tell me what the difference is between a Muslim terrorist and a Christian fundamentalist who stated that 9/11 happened because "God has punished America"?

Reverend Jerry Falwell

"God continues to lift the curtain and allow the enemies of America to give us probably what we deserve... The abortionists have got to bear some burden for this because God will not be mocked. And when we destroy 40 million little innocent babies, we make God mad. I really believe that the pagans, and the abortionists, and the feminists, and the gays and the lesbians who are actively trying to make that an alternative lifestyle, the ACLU, People for the American Way — all of them who have tried to secularize America — I point the finger in their face and say, 'You helped this happen.'" (9/13/2001)

Maybe there isn't much difference, though they would hardly seem to be the same. Both cloak themselves in the authoritative robes of religion to voice their opinion of how life should be led. Both desire to impose the "right" doctrine, which is immune to the influence of modern society.

To them change is not progress. It is a threat to a golden age that never really existed. It is an evil to be resisted at all costs.

Many Muslim theologians around the world enforce a 12th-century interpretation of the Koran. They consider this view as holy as the word of God itself.

Shouldn't Allah's words be read anew in the context of a constantly evolving society, one much different than that a millennium ago?

Is it right that some parts of verses are remembered and others just forgotten? Like Sura 4:3, which states that "a man may have four wives." But why is the next clause ignored: "however, if you cannot be equally just, then you must have just one"?

[Celeste: In the Koran, Sura 4:3 states, "If you fear that you will not be able to act justly towards orphans [who are to be the first choice in marriage, then instead of them] marry two, three, or four of such women as seem good to you, but if you fear you will not be equitable, then [marry] only one, or what your right hands own [as slaves]. Thus it will be more likely that you will not be partial."]

Just like you and I are talking, all Afghani women need to be able to speak their minds.

Women must be more than simply housewives.

They should be free to vote, govern, play public roles, and pursue any career they choose or are capable of.

Feudal prejudices shackle both our cultures. How in any land can half the population be treated as passive and silent? Mothers have more to contribute than just bearing children, cooking, and cleaning. Daughters have more value than being mere chattel.

Being taken for granted is one thing. A woman's ability to work, vote, and be treated equally under the law were once seen as impossible in America only a century ago. You see, things can change if we want them to.

Now is the time for us to assert our rights as individuals.

As citizens it is our duty to help build and shape a more just society.

The sun needs to shine on our sisters' faces. We can no longer afford to let our voices be veiled.

For our sake and for theirs, we must speak out for change.

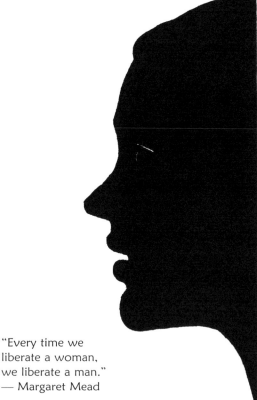

"Every time we liberate a woman, we liberate a man."
— Margaret Mead

11th Grade History — Mr. Pearson: Class Report

Name: Hector Gonzalez
Born: Hayward, California, 1985

My parents say school isn't the real world. They tell me that I should enjoy being a student as long as I can until I can't avoid the working world any longer. It's funny they say that, since I'm at the restaurant almost as much as they are.

But I understand what they're getting at. I'd like to go to college since my parents didn't have the chance. My older brother Ramon didn't bother. He's a mechanic and makes a pretty good living. But my parents want me and my sister Hilda to get a degree. So I promised them that I would give it a shot.

But school doesn't seem like a different place to me. It's not sheltered like adults think. School has a lot of the same pressures. Classes can be interesting or busy, or challenging one minute and really boring the next. There's always some sort of test or exam coming up, but it's easy to get distracted. Kids smoke, drink, and do drugs just like their parents do at home. They carry protection — knives mostly, but occasionally guns. People want to impress each other, to dress fine, and drive nice cars. To get spending money, they take from their parents or hold down side jobs. To me, that's how life is.

The cliques are there: the popular crowd, jocks, nerds, geeks, dopers, and homies. The same gangs that are on the street are in the halls.

I play football, so I see the same things there. In sports, we have these old rivalries with other schools. When you think of it, they're kinda pointless. They're created as an excuse so we can have an enemy to fight against. I could've easily gone to Mount Washington or Roosevelt High, and I have friends that do. So it's not like I have any reason to hate them except when I'm on the field and they're on the other side.

Running clears my mind and lets me focus.

There my coach tells me to knock my opponent down, and I do it. Nothing personal. Just following orders. It's just dumb luck that I'm not on their team. In that way, school seems pretty much like the rest of the world.

Anyway, Caleb Lipman came into our place to eat one day. We serve Mexican food, even though my dad is an El Salvadoran cook and my mom is a Costa Rican hostess. Go figure. As I took his order, I noticed I hadn't seen him before. I asked him if it was his first time here. Caleb said it was. He walked by all the time, and today he decided to give us a try.

For an old white dude, he was nicer than I expected. He treated me like I was his amigo, not a waiter. I suggested he try our enchiladas and he was cool with that. Since it wasn't that busy, we sat down together while my dad prepped his meal. We got to talking. He's a character who has a lot to say. He gave me a lot to think about. Like maybe we should be learning something no matter where we're at.

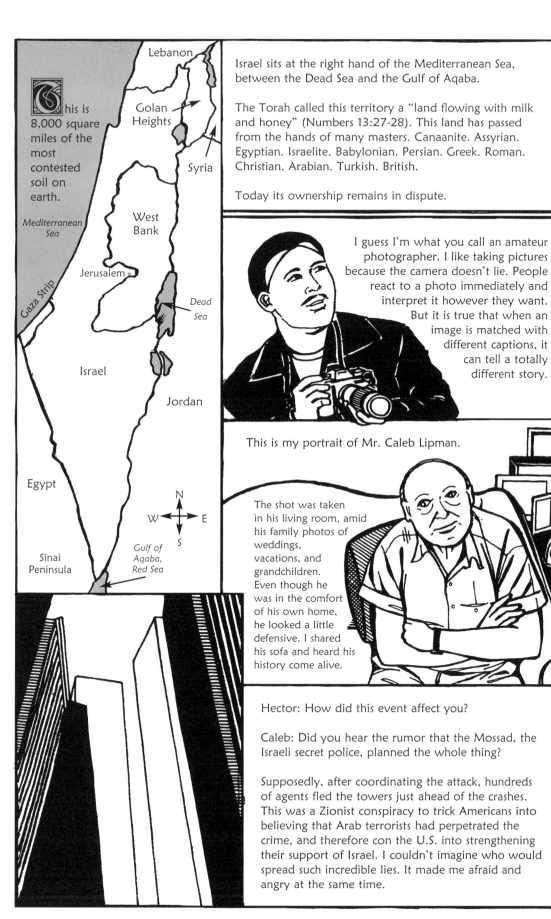

This is 8,000 square miles of the most contested soil on earth.

Lebanon

Golan Heights

Syria

West Bank

Jerusalem *

Dead Sea

Mediterranean Sea

Gaza Strip

Israel

Jordan

Egypt

Sinai Peninsula

Gulf of Aqaba, Red Sea

N
W — E
S

Israel sits at the right hand of the Mediterranean Sea, between the Dead Sea and the Gulf of Aqaba.

The Torah called this territory a "land flowing with milk and honey" (Numbers 13:27-28). This land has passed from the hands of many masters. Canaanite. Assyrian. Egyptian. Israelite. Babylonian. Persian. Greek. Roman. Christian. Arabian. Turkish. British.

Today its ownership remains in dispute.

I guess I'm what you call an amateur photographer. I like taking pictures because the camera doesn't lie. People react to a photo immediately and interpret it however they want. But it is true that when an image is matched with different captions, it can tell a totally different story.

This is my portrait of Mr. Caleb Lipman.

The shot was taken in his living room, amid his family photos of weddings, vacations, and grandchildren. Even though he was in the comfort of his own home, he looked a little defensive. I shared his sofa and heard his history come alive.

Hector: How did this event affect you?

Caleb: Did you hear the rumor that the Mossad, the Israeli secret police, planned the whole thing?

Supposedly, after coordinating the attack, hundreds of agents fled the towers just ahead of the crashes. This was a Zionist conspiracy to trick Americans into believing that Arab terrorists had perpetrated the crime, and therefore con the U.S. into strengthening their support of Israel. I couldn't imagine who would spread such incredible lies. It made me afraid and angry at the same time.

Many years ago, when I was a soldier in the Israeli Self-Defense forces, I learned the martial art of Krav Maga. Last week, I noticed they now teach a class in Fremont.

Speaking of this art of self-defense, former Israeli Prime Minister Shimon Peres once said:

"The two greatest dangers in the world today are waged by missiles (and missiles do not respect borders), and knife fights (since terrorism does not respect borders either)."

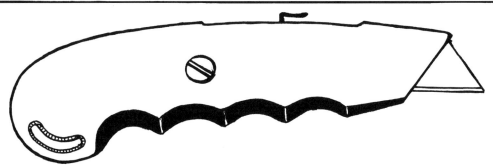

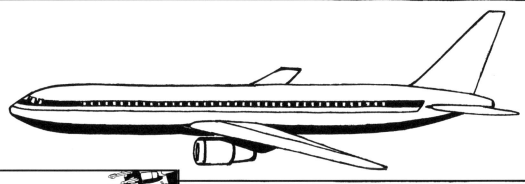

His prescience was uncanny. A few men with boxcutters transformed passenger jetliners into living warheads.

Some armchair scientists have calculated that the energy from the explosions of those four planes was one-tenth the magnitude of the nuclear bomb that destroyed Hiroshima in World War II.

Whatever the case, this atrocity has ushered in a new and more terrible phase of conflict in the Middle East, for all around the world to see. Suddenly war is waged as much for the cameras and people living at home as it is by those on the streets. For both it is live and a memory.

But the reality always can be disputed, depending on which way you look at it.

Israel and I were born in the aftermath of World War II. It was forged in war, a condition that it still finds itself in today. Granted "the mandate of Palestine" by the League of Nations in 1922, Israel declared its independence and the British ended their protection on May 14, 1948.

1948: War of Independence.

David Ben-Gurion (1886–1973)
Founding Father and Prime Minister

The next day it was attacked by the armies of Egypt, Jordan, Syria, Lebanon, and Saudi Arabia. Israel survived. Arab nations tried to boycott Israel economically. Then came the 1956 Sinai War.

Moshe Dayan (1915–1981)
Minister of Defense

1967: Six-Day War

A decade later, Israel preemptively attacked and destroyed the air forces of Egypt, Syria, and Jordan, and then occupied Egypt's Sinai Peninsula, Jordan's West Bank, and Syria's Golan Heights.

Golda Meir
(1898–1978)
Premier

1973: Yom Kippur War

Seeking revenge six years later, President Anwar Sadat's Egyptian army invaded Israel over the Suez Canal and Syrians overran the Golan Heights. Sixteen days later a cease-fire was declared.

1982: Invasion of Lebanon

A decade later, Israel pushed to Beirut to battle the Palestinian Liberation Organization (PLO) and Syrian-supported factions. The U.S. Army came in as a peacekeeping force, but eventually withdrew after over 200 Marines were killed by attacks from suicide bombers.

Now with this Palestinian Intifada, we have descended another level in this downward spiral of violence.

The PLO's mercurial Yasser Arafat clings to power on one side. The Likud's hardline Ariel Sharon on the other.

Now we have checkpoints and travel restrictions. Fences and armed guards. Barbed wire and barriers. Walls and watchtowers. Occupied lands and sealed ghettoes.

Distrustful neighbors live fretfully under a contant stage of seige.

Round-the-clock surveillance and paranoia have become commonplace. The security police forces never rest, nor do those who plot against them underground.

Is it anti-Semitic to say that Israel is handling the Palestinians like the Nazis treated the Jews? Part of me says yes absolutely — it is blasphemy. But another part says, God help us all if that is true.

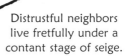

Hector: The U.S. gives Israel over $3 billion annually, one-sixth of the total for all of America's foreign aid. Is this the right use of it?

Caleb: I agree with those who say that when a nation's livelihood is at stake, it has the right to act in self-defense.

But it is also true that we have been desensitized by mind-numbing violence. Atrocities fall on each side. Lionized by one. Ignored by the other. And vice versa.

Both the powerful and the powerless face the same dilemma. Frustration leads to despair. Shock leads to callousness. Finally, futility breeds contempt, which is the deadliest poison to hope itself.

Hector: Why is this so much about turf?

Caleb: This is the problem everywhere. Jerusalem is a unique place in all the world since it is a holy site to three religions.

This is cause for both great celebration but also eternal conflict.

The Jews have the Temple Mount, the site where the First and Second Temples stood.

The Wailing Wall marks part of the Temple's old border. Jews believe the Messiah will arrive here when their redemption ultimately comes.

Of course, Christians believe that this already took place at this very spot.

This is the road where Jesus Christ walked on his way to be crucified. The Via Dolorosa. The "Way of Sorrows."

Jesus was judged by Pontius Pilate and then carried his cross westward to Calvary where he died between two common criminals. Easter commemorates his resurrection three days later. On the other hand, the Muslims call the same site Haram al-Sharif or the "Noble Sanctuary." Here is the Dome of the Rock, built to honor the prophet Muhammad's Night Journey. Here also is the al-Aqsa Mosque, Islam's third-holiest site, where the Koran states Muhammad ascended into heaven. Jerusalem is the intersection of politics, land, and faith. It's a mess without a traffic cop.

Hector: Do you think there will ever be peace?

Perhaps some day. I hope.

My son Bruce told me how he met a colleague recently at a trade convention.

They kissed, shared a cup of coffee, and reminisced.

Bruce asked about a telltale mark on her face. It was a scar caused by a stray bullet.

Fadwa was an attractive forty-year-old Lebanese woman, whose memories of war could never go away.

Bruce wondered why Fadwa, after traveling through Europe and America, had returned to live in Beirut. She said, "I had to go back.

It was my home. I will live or die there, for better or for worse. Hopefully I can help make a difference."

Bruce told her, "You and I are the same. Others don't know what we've been through. We two, we are brother and sister." With a hug, they agreed their culture and spirit made them...

more closely related than different.

It's funny. Bruce wasn't as intimate even with those he shared a kibbutz with.

When my son was your age, he lived on a commune for a year. Like many Americans, he thought that by working the land he would get in touch with his ancestral roots. Instead he just confronted the modern justifications for an ancient ethnic feud.

I've come to see that the lives of Arabs and Jews are both intertwined. They won't go away and neither will we.

Ultimately we need to share this land together, to have space for each of us to live in and call our own.

Peace is possible, if only people want to heal a shared wound badly enough.

11th Grade History — Mr. Pearson: Class Report
Name: Valerie Silverberg
Born: Englewood Cliffs, New Jersey, 1986

I was born across the Hudson River from New York and my family lived in Manhattan when I was a baby. Naturally I don't remember too much from when I was that young. But my parents told me they moved because they thought Manhattan was too crowded and busy a place to raise a kid.

My dad is an architect, so he said he always wanted to live somewhere that still had room for him to help fill up. My mom is a journalist, and she said she just wanted a bigger house. So we came to California when I was 2 and have been here ever since.

I'm a third-generation American. My two sets of grandparents emigrated from Austria and Poland before the start of World War II. They were lucky to leave in time, since a lot of their relatives didn't make it out. Back then they were Orthodox, but now my family practices Reformed Judaism.

Most of the time, I don't think of myself in religious terms. My older brother Josh says that being Jewish can be more of an ethnicity than a practicing belief. But people always need labels to call other people. It's human nature to try to categorize what they see when they see it. When strangers hear my name, I can tell some think they automatically know who I am, where I'm from, or what I believe.

I'm sure I do it too — I mean, judge other people. But I try not to. Everyone is different. Or at least they can be. I try to let my actions speak for me, and then others can think what they want to.

My dad's office often works with a bunch of contractors who are Middle Eastern. Given all the horror stories from Israel and Palestine, you'd imagine they wouldn't get along. But somehow they don't let politics get between them. Mohammad Mustafa works on-site with my dad to construct buildings. I've met

I enjoy being the editor of the school paper.

him before, and he told me it's important to work with people you trust. When my dad told Mohammad about my assignment, he said his brother Ahmed would be a good person to talk to, if I was up to it.

Even though I've read about Egyptians so many times in the Bible, and seen them in *The Ten Commandments* and *The Prince of Egypt*, I've never really had an in-depth discussion with one before. Politics can get too personal and nasty, so I was a little nervous before I spoke with Ahmed.

I may not agree with everything that Ahmed had to say, but that's not a bad thing. It's like in speech and debate class where there are arguments and counter arguments. That's what I like, the chance to take turns, state the pros and cons, and use reason and the facts to make the best case. However, in life there isn't always a judge who will award points to decide the winner. Most of the time, we're left on our own and we just have to sort things out between ourselves.

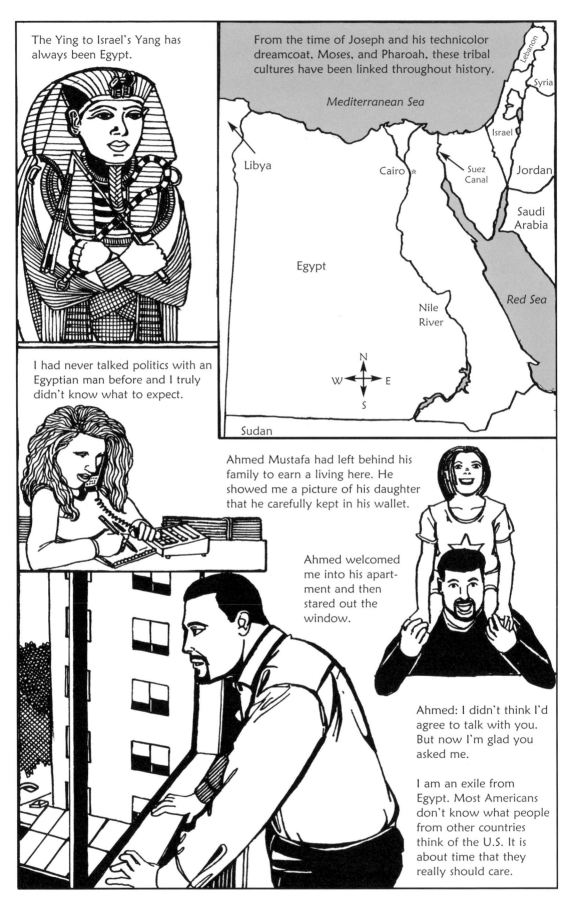

The Ying to Israel's Yang has always been Egypt.

From the time of Joseph and his technicolor dreamcoat, Moses, and Pharoah, these tribal cultures have been linked throughout history.

Lebanon

Syria

Mediterranean Sea

Libya

Israel

Cairo ✳

Suez Canal

Jordan

Saudi Arabia

Egypt

Nile River

Red Sea

N
W E
S

Sudan

I had never talked politics with an Egyptian man before and I truly didn't know what to expect.

Ahmed Mustafa had left behind his family to earn a living here. He showed me a picture of his daughter that he carefully kept in his wallet.

Ahmed welcomed me into his apartment and then stared out the window.

Ahmed: I didn't think I'd agree to talk with you. But now I'm glad you asked me.

I am an exile from Egypt. Most Americans don't know what people from other countries think of the U.S. It is about time that they really should care.

Just in this past hundred years, Egypt and its Arab neighbors have gone from states with few resources to some of the richest nations on Earth.

All because of one thing.

Oil.

Oil is a modern phenomenon. Before oil, there were no cars, or planes, or motorized boats. People traveled by their own sweat or via animals. Then they harnessed the power of the wind, wood, steam, and coal.

Born in this century, we take this for granted. The exploration and storage of gas is the foundation for travel and trade. We exploit it heedlessly and have erected a maze of industries that at every mile make gas as available and cheap as water.

But oil won't last forever. In less than two centuries, humans will have exhausted the fossil fuel reserves that took the Earth its lifetime to accumulate.

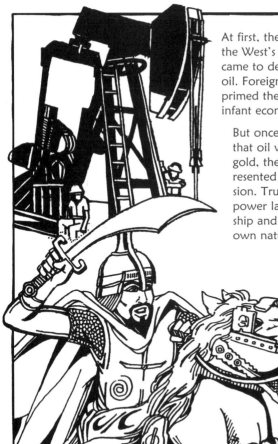

At first, the Arabs welcomed the West's attention when it came to developing their oil. Foreign investment primed the pumps of their infant economies.

But once they realized that oil was truly black gold, the Arabic nations resented the West's intrusion. True and lasting power lay in the ownership and control of their own natural resources.

Gamal Abdel-Nasser (1918–1970) helped overthrow the monarchy of King Farouk and the British colonialists in 1952. Two years later he seized power through a military coup and then presided over the transformation of Eygpt into the leader of the Arab nationalism movement.

Not since Saladin vanquished the Crusaders did Egypt have such a champion.

But after a series of wars, a new generation chose another direction.

President Carter sought peace in the Middle East and wanted America to be the mediator with the Camp David Accords.

So Eygpt's Anwar Sadat won the Nobel Peace Prize with Israel's leader Menachem Begin in 1978. But hated for his unforgivable betrayal to the despised Zionists, Sadat was assassinated by the militant Egyptian Islamic Jihad in 1981.

Seated beside Sadat at the Cairo military parade was Vice President Hosni Mubarak, when suddenly a cadre of armed soldiers turned their guns on the grandstand. Despite the hail of bullets, Mubarak suffered only a shot in the hand.

Succeeding the President, Mubarak immediately cracked down on any fundamentalist threats to ensure his political survival. Escaping his own assassination attempt in 1995, he was convinced that he needed to continue stifling political dissent and opposition even further.

Flush with $2 billion a year in U.S. aid, Mubarak can harass, imprison, and silence his critics with impunity.

Even academic moderates are too dangerous. Therefore Mubarak has jailed Dr. Saad Eddin Ibrahim, an advocate of democracy and free speech and co-founder of the Arab Human Rights Organization. The government closed his center that promoted political reform, voter education, election monitoring, and literacy campaigns.

[Valerie: Ibrahim said this after his previous arrest in 2000: "It is a test of whether Egypt's civil society can survive and thrive or will be muzzled and intimidated as suggested in the recent report of Amnesty International.... I am confident that a new generation of Egyptians will carry on that mission, knowing that democracy everywhere requires courage and vigilance."]

Thousands have been arrested, tortured, and "disappeared" without charges or trials. It's like spraying poison on weeds or insects. It makes the survivors much more resistant and harder to remove. Radicals get more extreme. This complete suppression of dissent has become a pressure cooker. As discontent grows, without a way to channel dissatisfaction. the lid is destined to blow.

الْقَاعِدَة

I WANT YOU FOR OUR JIHAD
NEAREST RECRUITING STATION

Of the terrorists, most come from Saudi Arabia, but many come from Egypt. In Arabic, Al Qaeda means "The Base" or "The Foundation." Its very name implies that it is the keystone of Islam and represents the spirit of true Muslims. This is how this extremist movement has drawn such grassroots support. Few are lucky like me and have the means to leave. Most are forced to imagine for themselves a new way life.

Getting an education but having no future creates a volatile brew. The young have no prospects for jobs, upward mobility, or political change in a society dominated by an entrenched hierarchy.

Mohamed Atta	Marwan Al-Shehhi	Ziad Samir Jarrah	Hani Hanjour

They see a selfish elite enriched by oil money, a habitually poor populace, and a superpower that supports Israel against Arab Muslims and controls holy lands with an armed occupation.

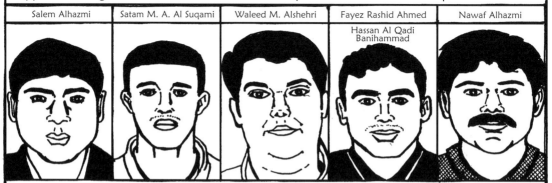

Salem Alhazmi	Satam M. A. Al Suqami	Waleed M. Alshehri	Fayez Rashid Ahmed Hassan Al Qadi Banihammad	Nawaf Alhazmi

With nowhere to go, they can only funnel their energy towards Allah and into imagining how society could and should be different. They chant "allah u akbar" as a rallying cry.

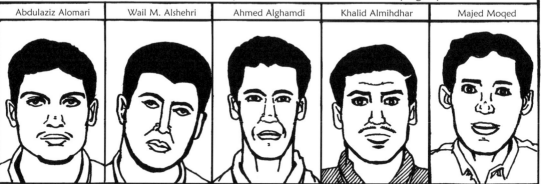

Abdulaziz Alomari	Wail M. Alshehri	Ahmed Alghamdi	Khalid Almihdhar	Majed Moqed

You may not believe it and I may not agree with it, but these terrorists have become heroes to millions of Muslims in Africa, Arabia, and Asia who see the U.S. as a supporter of their oppressors.

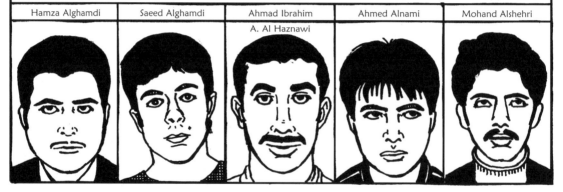

Hamza Alghamdi	Saeed Alghamdi	Ahmad Ibrahim A. Al Haznawi	Ahmed Alnami	Mohand Alshehri

I don't imagine that this was a statement they intended ...

but they used the oil that America so desperately craves against itself.

The terrorists crashed two 757s and two 767s. Altogether these planes held 60,000 gallons of jet fuel. It was like lighting four huge Molotov cocktails.

[Valerie: A car that gets 20 mpg and drives 10,000 miles a year uses 500 gallons annually. The four planes held enough fuel to last 120 cars a whole year of driving.

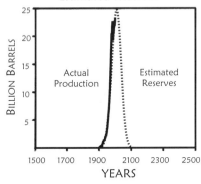

World Oil Production & Estimated Reserves

BILLION BARRELS

Actual Production — Estimated Reserves

YEARS

• With over 200 million registered vehicles in the U.S., the growth of auto registration is greater than that of the general population.

• Used for 80% of Americans' travel, cars and trucks consume nearly 75% of U.S. transportation energy.

• 40% of land in U.S. cities is related to operating, storing, and maintaining automobiles.

• Stuck in traffic for 1.6 million hours a year, Americans waste $40 billion in lost productivity and fuel.

One mile of new freeway costs $50 million to build.

Over its lifetime, an average car will release 34 tons of carbon dioxide and 300 pounds of smog-producing chemicals. Air pollution contributes to 60,000 American deaths annually.]

You would be surprised at how people view America.

Arabs do want freedom of speech,

U.S. tariffs on imported steel.

the ability to organize politically, fair elections, and economic development.

But they see an America supporting the persecution of Palestinians, strangling the citizens of Iraq with economic sanctions. People see this on TV every day.

People protest against the hypocrisy. America wants free trade but protects its own industries such as sugar, corn, and steel.

America proudly champions freedom and democracy but supports military dictators and only sabotages them when it seems more expedient.

IRAN — Reza Shah Pahlavi

PHILIPPINES — Ferdinand Marcos

PANAMA — Manuel Noriega

CHILE — Augusto Pinochet

SERBIA — Slobodan Milosevic

Americans consume most of the world's resources,

The Constitution

We the People

Bill of Rights

Congress of the United States,

... but America wants exemption from international law that enforces greater environmental responsibility.

America professes to be the land of the Bill of Rights and Declaration of Independence.

But its track record of putting those words into action has been less than consistent. If it were, attitudes overseas would be very different than they are today.

11th Grade History — Mr. Pearson: Class Report
Name: Wahid Zahir
Born: Islamabad, Pakistan, 1985

It's weird how neighbors can become the worst enemies. Back in Asia, I grew up believing that way about Indians. The Pakistani government constantly reinforced this idea and so did the newspapers and the TV. The Indians believed in the wrong gods, had awful leaders, and despised our existence. We had to be ready to defend ourselves and fight them at all costs. With a rifle, cannon, or even a nuclear bomb.

I came to America when I was nine. People found my name hard to pronounce, so they started calling me Wally instead. But what shocked me more was that people didn't know where I was from or thought I was Indian.

I would quickly tell them I was Pakistani but it didn't matter. At first I felt insulted. It was bad that they didn't know where Pakistan was. After a while I wondered whether Americans simply flunked geography. But it was worse that they mistook me for an Indian. Couldn't they tell the difference between us?

But then I thought Americans just didn't care. To be honest, most people can't tell Pakistanis and Indians apart. Even my parents can't most of the time. I mean, Pakistan only became a separate country in 1947, after the British left. But the differences we once thought were so important when we lived over there just weren't in America. Here, the old grudges didn't have to apply. People could just start over and call a truce. Or they could even be friends if they didn't bring the prejudices of the past with them.

Today, when people think I'm Indian, I don't mind as much as I used to. My younger brother and sister care even less. But recently, I've had more cases of mistaken identity...I've been called an Afghan or Arab. I can understand why they do it, but it doesn't make me feel any better. It actually feels worse, since they think I'm a threat to them when I'm not at all.

Your perspective depends on where you're coming from. I haven't been back to Pakistan

I enjoy meeting people when I work at the theater.

since I came here. But my parents still consider it home, and they promise that they will bring the family back to visit for summer vacation. There Pakistanis probably couldn't tell a German apart from an Australian or a Swede. I imagine how Caucasians in Asia could feel the same way I did here.

Beverly Odoms was watching a movie at the theater where I work. That's where we first met. On weekends, I operate the refreshments stand. She arrived early before the show started, and she ordered some popcorn. I mentioned that I had seen her come here before. Beverly said she was watching a lot of movies recently to get away from life.

I had heard that phrase before and asked her why. I remember she replied, "Sometimes life doesn't give you a choice." That's when I thought it would be interesting to hear her story.

Oakland is the biggest port in the Bay Area.

This is the .... ──── land of oaks.

Here's where ships come from every ocean, pass under the Golden Gate, and unload containers of all kinds.

This dockyard is a point of transition.

But as they say, the more things change, the more they stay the same.

Change is eternal. You can even hear it in a person's voice. But I've learned that you can't capture the tone of a person's voice just by writing down their words or taking a picture of their expressions. So I brought along a tape recorder with me.

Wahid: Ms. Odoms, please tell me a little bit about yourself.

Beverly: My name is Beverly Odoms. I'm 38 years old. I was in the ROTC, which helped put me through school. After I graduated from college, I spent the next five years in the Navy.

Since then, I've held down a lot of different positions. But now I'm a meter maid for the city. It's a job, but it beats being out of work. At least I get some sun and fresh air every day.

When I'm patrolling down on the street I like to say, "If you don't pay the time, you gotta do the fine."

Wahid: What was your life like here before 9/11?

Beverly: Well, the whole Internet boom passed me over. I saw the commotion over new buildings and expensive cars and fancy suits. The city bent over backwards to lure companies here, handing out tax breaks, and even selling the name of the stadium to the highest bidder.

A lot of it came and went, but some of the changes did indirectly affect me.

When the Yuppies started moving in, land values rose and they're still rising today.

Since City Hall needs to collect its due, property taxes kept rising. It got to the point that people couldn't even afford to stay in their own homes.

A lot of my neighbors cashed in to move somewhere cheaper and farther away. No point in fighting a war you can't win.

LIQUOR BEER

Sure, the neighborhood seems bad to new folks. But we've had to live with it all this time. They think the only way to fix it is to move us out. Some call that "gentrification." Other folks call it discrimination.

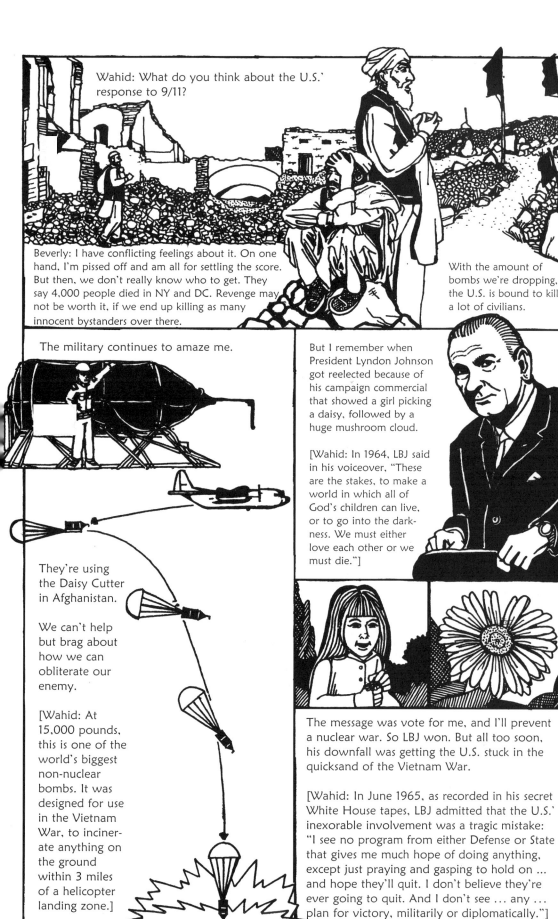

Wahid: What do you think about the U.S.' response to 9/11?

Beverly: I have conflicting feelings about it. On one hand, I'm pissed off and am all for settling the score. But then, we don't really know who to get. They say 4,000 people died in NY and DC. Revenge may not be worth it, if we end up killing as many innocent bystanders over there.

With the amount of bombs we're dropping, the U.S. is bound to kill a lot of civilians.

The military continues to amaze me.

But I remember when President Lyndon Johnson got reelected because of his campaign commercial that showed a girl picking a daisy, followed by a huge mushroom cloud.

[Wahid: In 1964, LBJ said in his voiceover, "These are the stakes, to make a world in which all of God's children can live, or to go into the darkness. We must either love each other or we must die."]

They're using the Daisy Cutter in Afghanistan.

We can't help but brag about how we can obliterate our enemy.

[Wahid: At 15,000 pounds, this is one of the world's biggest non-nuclear bombs. It was designed for use in the Vietnam War, to inciner-ate anything on the ground within 3 miles of a helicopter landing zone.]

The message was vote for me, and I'll prevent a nuclear war. So LBJ won. But all too soon, his downfall was getting the U.S. stuck in the quicksand of the Vietnam War.

[Wahid: In June 1965, as recorded in his secret White House tapes, LBJ admitted that the U.S.' inexorable involvement was a tragic mistake: "I see no program from either Defense or State that gives me much hope of doing anything, except just praying and gasping to hold on ... and hope they'll quit. I don't believe they're ever going to quit. And I don't see ... any ... plan for victory, militarily or diplomatically."]

Wahid: Do you have any doubts about the war?

Beverly: I'm still in the Reserves. So if this gets any worse, my number might get called. My family won't like it. If I stop working, I'll lose my salary. But I have an obligation to serve.

Still, I do have reservations about the whole situation. War never solves everything.

Even once you start, you don't always get the results you want. We won the Gulf War hands down. But Saddam's still there. Then G.I.s got Gulf War Syndrome. Today we're more dependent on oil than ever before. And some car company turned the Hummer into a gas-guzzling SUV status symbol.

Now we're gonna get knee-deep in Afghanistan. Did you know they're the world's biggest growers of opium poppies? The Taliban had clamped down, but once we get rid of them, the farmers will go right back to it.

Wahid: How does that affect us?

Beverly: What about the war on drugs? It's not working. Never will. But it's a harsh reality on my block every day.

We don't need to go looking to clean up somebody else's mess.

The war zone is here in our own backyard.

Colors are what it's all about. It's about what side you're on. The dealers are the capitalists. They're entrepreneurs just like the alcohol and cigarette companies.

Their best customers are addicts, so they keep making new products:

Crack. Crank. Smack.

Then there's Dope, Eck, and Oxycotton.

They shift alliances and undercut the competition, all to protect their racket.

Drive-bys hit the front pages for a day. Most of the time, victims don't even get an obituary. TV has it all wrong. Guns aren't glamorous or dramatic. It's just kids killing kids. You wish it was a movie so you could turn it off. But you can't.

At their funerals, their friends can only do a death dance for them. The only memorial they get is what their crew wears on their backs.

[Wahid: In 2001 Oakland had 87 homicides. Its homicide rate of 21.8 per 100,000 residents was greater than the rates for England, Germany, Japan, France, and the United States combined. In 2002, Oakland's homicide rate climbed 25%.]

JAMAAL DRUMMOND 1976-2002

RIPeace 4EVER

I know the police gotta do their job, but on the streets we're black and they're white.

I've said goodbye to too many childhood friends. They're either dead or locked in the joint. Now with the "three strikes you're out" law, you can do 25 years to life for shoplifting candy.

[Wahid: I looked it up and Ms. Odoms was right about prisons:
• California spends more money on penitentiaries every year than on schools.
• The U.S. has more prisoners than Russia and has 25% of the world's total.
• Blacks make up 12% of the U.S. population but almost 50% of all inmates. A black boy has a 30% chance of being imprisoned during his lifetime. There are more black men in prison than in college. Over 70% of illegal drug users are white, but almost 60% of those arrested are black. In 1997, murder with a gun was the leading cause of death for black men ages 15-34. The same trends hold true for Latinos.]

America has had its fair share of homegrown psychos. Crazy cults and their charismatic leaders.

Charles Manson — 1960s

Jim Jones — 1970s

David Koresh — 1990s

Timothy McVeigh

Eric Harris

Dylan Klebod

But nowadays any disgruntled former soldier or even a vengeful high schooler who can get his hands on a gun and pull the trigger can become instant terrorists.

They say that Dylan Klebod imagined he would hijack a plane ...

and fly it into a building too.

What they did at Columbine was inexcusable, and there was hell to pay.

I don't admire what those two did, but I do understand it.

In a way, these kids are in the same hole as those terrorists. Picked on and pushed too far. Feeling too much hatred with no place to put it. No one's told me how we're going to cope with that.

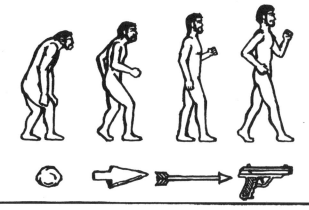

When your back is against a dead end, you come out swinging and damn the consequences.

If you're willing to die for your beliefs, right or wrong, and take others down with you, believe me, it's not a game anymore.

You use whatever you can get your hands on. A rock, a knife, a gun ... anything. It's like a perverse progression of human evolution.

Wahid: Do you have any last comments on the situation we're in today?

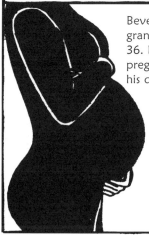

Beverly: My cousin's a grandfather and he's only 36. He got his girlfriend pregnant at 17 and now his daughter is expecting.

Now what kind of world is that baby going to be born into?

All I can say is that it's our responsibility to leave the world to our children a better place than we came into it. But the way things are looking, we have a big job ahead of us.

11th Grade History — Mr. Pearson: Class Report
Name: Phillip Tran
Born: Pasadena, California, 1986

I am the third of four children, with two older sisters and a younger brother. My parents fled Vietnam in 1975 right after the Viet Cong overthrew the South Vietnamese government. Since 1867, Vietnam had been a French colony. But in 1945, America recruited Ho Chi Minh, who was using Communism to protest against French rule, to equip a nationalist army to battle Japan.

After the end of World War II, Ho Chi Minh immediately declared an independent Vietnam based in the northern city of Hanoi, thereby dividing the nation. In 1954 he defeated the French, the first time a colonial power ever had been conquered militarily. As the Cold War with the Soviet Union intensified, the U.S. decided it could not let Communists control all of Vietnam. However, after a decade of fighting the Viet Cong, the U.S. finally pulled out of a losing war and guaranteed the South's collapse. My grandfather was a sergeant in the Southern army, so if his family didn't escape, they all would've been killed.

When the capital of Saigon fell, my mother and father were teenagers and didn't even know each other. My mom's family managed to make their way to a refugee camp in Thailand. My dad's family became boat people and fled to Hong Kong.

After coming to America, my parents met during junior high school in Monterey Park, down in Southern California.

Certainly, I haven't had to endure the hardships that my parents or grandparents went through. It's difficult for me to consider traveling halfway around the world to rebuild my life from scratch. Let alone take my children, siblings, and parents.

Often my parents will scold us and tell us to not take things for granted. We've gotten used to hearing this and dutifully nod our heads. But they never tell us in detail what really happened over there. Whenever I see a documentary on PBS, I ask them whether they were there and

Sometimes I wonder how lucky I am to be here.

recall those events. Then it's their turn to nod and quickly change the subject. Old memories still can be too painful.

So, the stories about the people who died at the World Trade Center really hit home with me. Too often we forget the people who labor in the shadows. After reading their obituaries, I realized that they were just like my parents. Struggling to get here and to stay here and to make a new life. Sending their paychecks home to support their families overseas, they just wanted to work hard and get ahead.

I bumped into Victor Yanilov totally by accident. A few weekends ago, I was in San Francisco with some friends. We were killing time before going to see a movie, so we decided to drop in a Russian bakery. I had never been in one before and now it seems there are a lot of them. The Russian population in the Bay Area has exploded in the past few years.

Since I know practically everyone my parents know, I thought it would be easier to just ask somebody off the street. Victor was minding his business, drinking his coffee at a table. I didn't know who he was, or if he spoke English at all. So I just walked up and asked him if I could discuss 9/11 with him for school project. Funny, he seemed like he had been waiting for this chance for a long time. Looking back, I'm not surprised at all that he said yes. I guess we both have a lot in common. We were both at the right place at the right time.

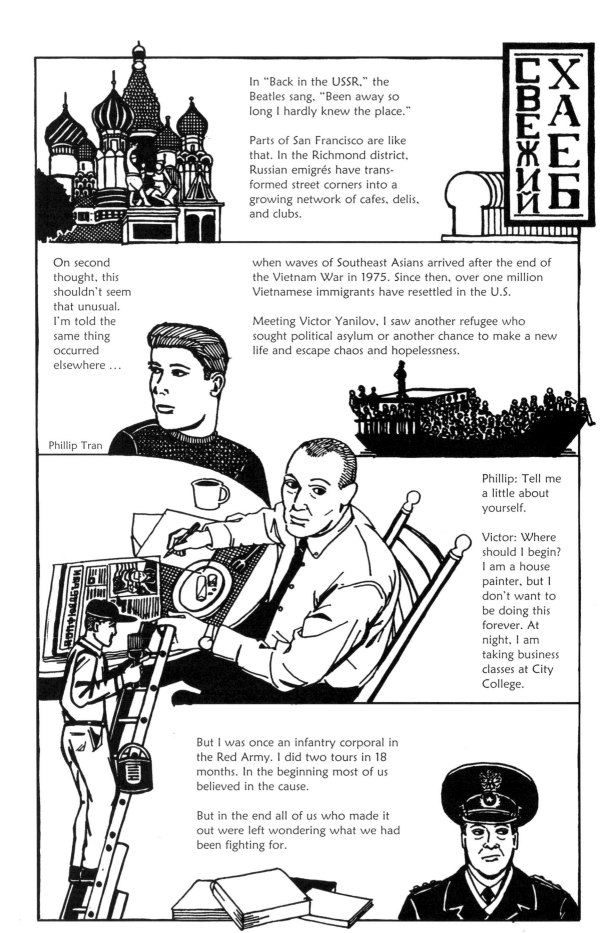

In "Back in the USSR," the Beatles sang, "Been away so long I hardly knew the place."

Parts of San Francisco are like that. In the Richmond district, Russian emigrés have transformed street corners into a growing network of cafes, delis, and clubs.

СВЕЖИЙ ХЛЕБ

On second thought, this shouldn't seem that unusual. I'm told the same thing occurred elsewhere ...

Phillip Tran

when waves of Southeast Asians arrived after the end of the Vietnam War in 1975. Since then, over one million Vietnamese immigrants have resettled in the U.S.

Meeting Victor Yanilov, I saw another refugee who sought political asylum or another chance to make a new life and escape chaos and hopelessness.

Phillip: Tell me a little about yourself.

Victor: Where should I begin? I am a house painter, but I don't want to be doing this forever. At night, I am taking business classes at City College.

But I was once an infantry corporal in the Red Army. I did two tours in 18 months. In the beginning most of us believed in the cause.

But in the end all of us who made it out were left wondering what we had been fighting for.

What has been your reaction to 9/11?

No one could have expected it, but the U.S. government certainly received a lot of clues before it happened.

The saying is "the enemy of my enemy is my friend," no? The irony is obvious. The U.S. is fighting those whom they once helped to defeat Russia. And now Russia is America's ally.

Phillip: What are your personal experiences with war?

Victor: My friends and I wasted our youth in Afghanistan.

The domino theory worked both ways. After a series of failed Afghan revolutions, in 1979 Leonid Brezhnev propped up a government favorable to Russia.

The West only saw Communism expanding.

Jimmy Carter threatened to boycott the 1980 Moscow Olympics unless "Soviet invasion forces" withdrew from Afghanistan. We did not.

Carter's successor, Ronald Reagan, seized the role of a lifetime. In order to defeat the godless totalitarians, he promised that "the forces of good ultimately rally and triumph over evil."

If Rambo could single-handedly rescue America's wounded pride from both the theaters of Vietnam and Afghanistan ...

surely this ex-movie star could do the same.

Life goes by so fast. Twenty years ago seems like yesterday, when I was drafted to help suppress the Afghanis who resisted the Russian occupation.

We had all the desired advantages. Armor. Airpower. Artillery. Trained infantry. We had overwhelming military superiority.

Our generals thought we would pacify the Afghan rebels quite quickly.

Unfortunately they were wrong. No one had counted on a stubborn guerrilla war that would sap both our patience and morale.

Seeking all help possible, the Muslim mujahadeen invoked a jihad, a "holy war." They summoned thousands of Islam's true believers from around the world to come help them fight the accursed infidels who had invaded their homeland. Come they did.

But aid also came from unexpected sources.

The CIA pledged $700 million a year in a covert operation to instruct and equip "Afghan freedom fighters," just as they funded other anti-Communist insurgencies across the globe.

U.S. Stinger missiles proved more than a symbol of American support when they destroyed our helicopters and killed our comrades.

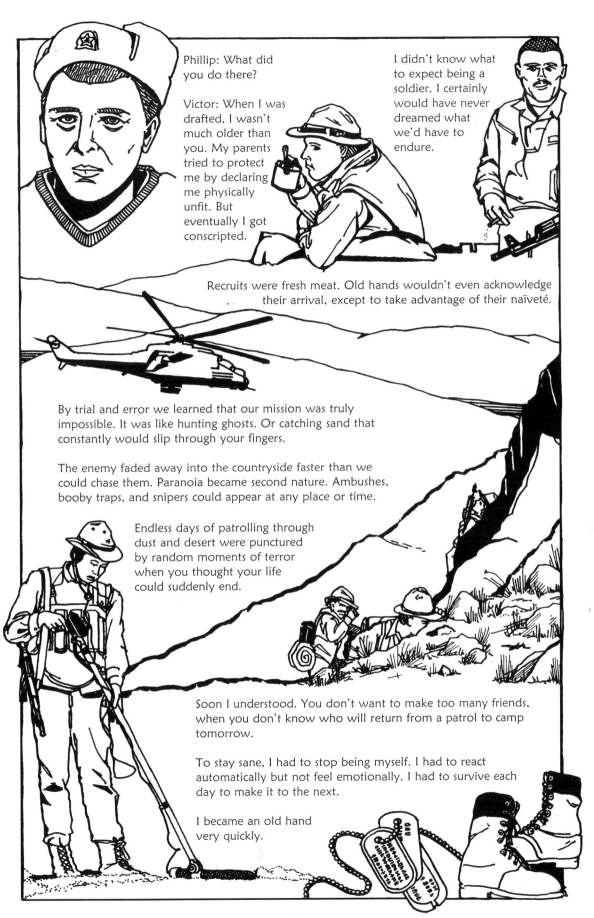

Phillip: What did you do there?

Victor: When I was drafted, I wasn't much older than you. My parents tried to protect me by declaring me physically unfit. But eventually I got conscripted.

I didn't know what to expect being a soldier. I certainly would have never dreamed what we'd have to endure.

Recruits were fresh meat. Old hands wouldn't even acknowledge their arrival, except to take advantage of their naïveté.

By trial and error we learned that our mission was truly impossible. It was like hunting ghosts. Or catching sand that constantly would slip through your fingers.

The enemy faded away into the countryside faster than we could chase them. Paranoia became second nature. Ambushes, booby traps, and snipers could appear at any place or time.

Endless days of patrolling through dust and desert were punctured by random moments of terror when you thought your life could suddenly end.

Soon I understood. You don't want to make too many friends, when you don't know who will return from a patrol to camp tomorrow.

To stay sane, I had to stop being myself. I had to react automatically but not feel emotionally. I had to survive each day to make it to the next.

I became an old hand very quickly.

Phillip: Then what happened?

Victor: The Afghan government had little popular support. Neither did the Russians. We did not expect this to be our Vietnam. A political quagmire. A lost decade.

It's no wonder that the U.S. President Richard Nixon once considered nuking North Vietnam just to get the whole thing over with. He settled for bombing Cambodia and Laos instead, to no avail.

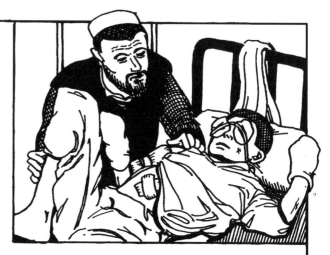

Unlike the Viet Cong, the Afghan guerrillas would never win. But in the same way, they just would never ever go away. And so popular support for the war in the Soviet Union declined, as the number of our boys returning in body bags kept increasing.

What does a soldier know about politics? Our job is just to do what we're told. To keep our heads down and fight whomever our leaders tell us is the enemy. Before landing in Kabul, I had never seen an Afghani before in my life. When I finally got on my transport for the flight back to the Soviet Union, I hoped I would never see another one as long as I lived.

So on May 15, 1988, they pulled the plug. Premier Mikhail Gorbachev ordered the recall of 115,000 Soviet soldiers. It was too late for many of us. Their final resting places were hundreds of miles from home.

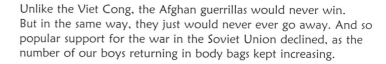

Moscow's Tomb of the Unknown Soldier.

[Phillip: 15,000 men had died, and the USSR soon was to fall apart, wracked by a decaying economy and divisive separatist movements.

It was worse for the Afghans. A million of them had died. Over 6 million more became refugees, which doubled the world's total at the time.]

Phillip: In Vietnam, my parents lived through the same type of tragedy. They fought to survive a disintegrating society, and then starvation and homelessness. When they finally made it safely here they had a hard time coping with normal life. Did you feel the same way?

Victor: Da. When I came home, no one understood what I had gone through. No one seemed to care.

But I just couldn't simply forget all that happened and pick up where I left off.

I was raised to be proud of my country. We were a superpower with a nuclear arsenal equal to the U.S. But here we couldn't defeat a ragtag bunch of farmers and teenagers who were willing to die for their beliefs and their land.

Our hearts weren't in it.

It wasn't a "just" war that galvanized a people's patriotism, like the epic defense of Leningrad against the Germans.

So when we returned home, we received little fanfare, and even less of a future.

No victory parades.
No satisfaction.
No closure.

We were called Afghanistis, the lost generation. We were the embarrassing reminders of a lost cause.

Only after I came here did I realize that there were Americans who shared my grief. For you, now more Vietnam vets have died after the war than were killed in it. But the wounds are still fresh.

The people fleeing the towers reminded me of the massacre at Mai Lai, like it occurred yesterday.

It is happening all over again in the republic of Chechnya. The same military problem. The same tarnished patriotism. The same human suffering.

I feel sorry for the poor souls sent there. It's another unresolvable border dispute and another bloody mess. It is sad to think that no lasting lessons were gained from our sacrifice.

Premier Vladimir Putin

Phillip: So what do you think of the U.S. invading Afghanistan?

Victor: Americans have always felt safe from harm. War is something they read about. Something that happens elsewhere. But with 9/11, the horrors of war finally came to American soil.

America's response was to bring the war back to them. But can they find the culprits without losing themselves? Now America will occupy the land we left in disgrace. I don't know why the U.S. would want to ignore our mistakes or theirs.

Life is too short to repeat the same tragedies if you can help it. In the long run, it seems to be better that way.

11th Grade History — Mr. Pearson: Class Report
Name: Xavier Frazier
Born: Richmond, California, 1986

I'm a Sagittarius but I don't believe in astrology too much. However, my mom does and she says I live up to my sign. She reads the horoscopes religiously every day, which I think funny since we all attend church every Sunday. Mom says it's like her morning cup of coffee, something she depends on to get her started.

Personally, I don't pay attention to that stuff. People say that I'm honest, direct, and that I try to find the truth. I've never picked up a bow and arrow in my life, but from what I know, I suppose I have what it takes. As the oldest child, I feel responsible to set as good an example as I can.

My dad grew up in Detroit, Michigan, the automobile capital of the world. My mom is from Des Plaines, Illinois, right outside Chicago. My parents moved out here for work, since the economy in the Midwest wasn't so good in the '80s. I was born just a little north of here, and we moved down to Fremont when my dad got a job at a local car dealership and didn't want to drive so far. My mom looks after my younger sisters at home and works part-time as an office manager.

At our new house, Mr. Nakamoto was our gardener for a long time. But he retired a few years ago, and then he passed away just last year. It was a strange feeling hearing that, after seeing him every week for a decade. I had never met his wife Hope before. So my mom thought it would be a good idea to call her and see how she was doing.

On Tuesdays, Mr. Nakamoto would come by our place in his pickup truck. He'd wear a pith helmet, sunglasses, and big canvas gloves. He'd have a neatly trimmed moustache and look like he was ready to go on a safari or something. He'd start on his hands and knees, cleaning up weeds from our front yard, and then mow the lawn in the back. In an hour he'd be done and on his way. Even though it would be hot and

I've learned that apple picking is fun but hard work.

dirty outside, I never heard him complain. I never knew much about him. I didn't even know his first name. I always called him Mr. Nakamoto.

If I wasn't doing anything special, I'd watch him through the window. I'd watch the way he trained plants to grow in certain directions and shapes. To me, a good gardener would make a good barber. Mr. Nakamoto would look at a bush from all sides before he'd start trimming. Even though he didn't mean to, he taught me the value of concentration, patience, and practice.

When I'd be home in the summertime, he'd often take a break. My mom would give him a cold glass of water and he'd flag me down. We'd rap about how the Raiders or the A's were doing. Often he'd give me an apple. They'd be ones that you couldn't get at the regular supermarket. I liked the Fujis the best. It was a special treat and he really enjoyed it when I ate it right in front of him.

He never told me why he gave me those presents, but now, after talking to Hope, I finally know. In his own way, he showed me how to do my best and to focus on the important things in life.

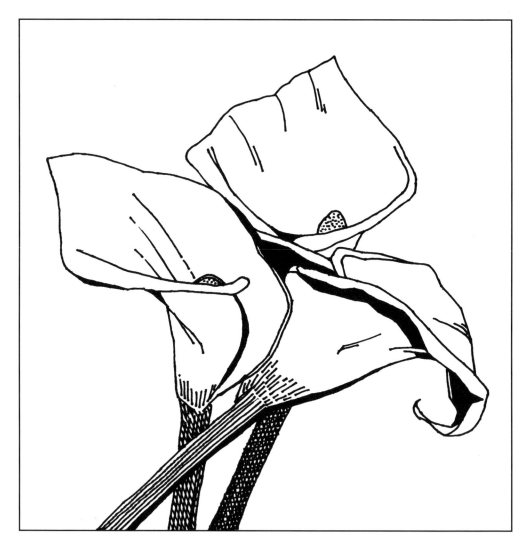

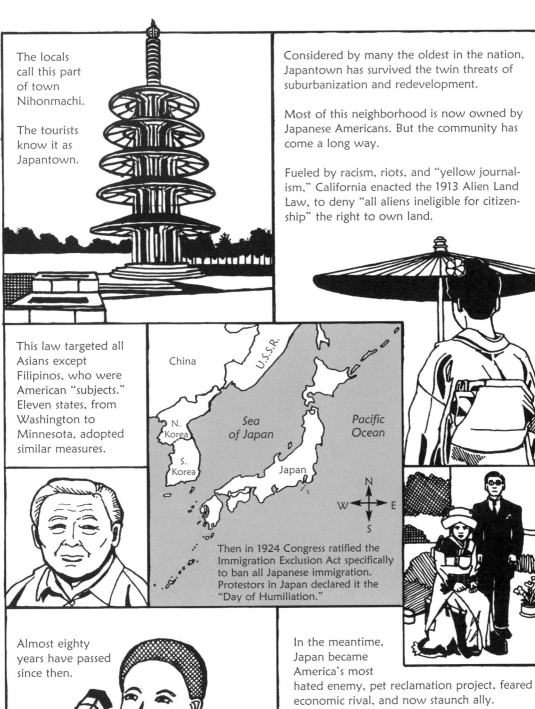

The locals call this part of town Nihonmachi.

The tourists know it as Japantown.

Considered by many the oldest in the nation, Japantown has survived the twin threats of suburbanization and redevelopment.

Most of this neighborhood is now owned by Japanese Americans. But the community has come a long way.

Fueled by racism, riots, and "yellow journalism," California enacted the 1913 Alien Land Law, to deny "all aliens ineligible for citizenship" the right to own land.

This law targeted all Asians except Filipinos, who were American "subjects." Eleven states, from Washington to Minnesota, adopted similar measures.

China

U.S.S.R.

N. Korea

S. Korea

Sea of Japan

Japan

Pacific Ocean

N
W   E
S

Then in 1924 Congress ratified the Immigration Exclusion Act specifically to ban all Japanese immigration. Protestors in Japan declared it the "Day of Humiliation."

Almost eighty years have passed since then.

In the meantime, Japan became America's most hated enemy, pet reclamation project, feared economic rival, and now staunch ally.

I borrowed a camcorder from my uncle so I could record my interview.

Here in Japantown I met Hope, the wife of Mr. Nakamoto. She and I sat down and ordered some tea. Then I pressed "record." I wanted to learn more about the life of a man I knew as our trusty and friendly gardener.

I was surprised to learn that I barely knew him at all.

Xavier: What did you think about that recent movie *Pearl Harbor*?

Hope: Well, it brought back a lot of bad memories, especially since it wasn't very accurate. For one thing, watching it you'd think Hawaii had no Asians at all, except for those rampaging Zero pilots.

I read that 9/11 had the highest American death toll since Pearl Harbor. It was 60 years ago, but it doesn't seem that far off when I think about it.

The country was caught by surprise. The first reaction was shock. Then fury. But we didn't expect the backlash to strike against us. After all, we were American citizens.

I was a teenager at the time. My parents were "Issei," first-generation Americans.

My mother Kyoko was a "picture bride" whose parents had arranged her marriage with my father Godai. Together they opened a grocery store in San Francisco and had four kids along the way.

I was the youngest child.

Franklin Delano Roosevelt is considered one of our greatest presidents ever. He was the first and only one to serve three terms in office. He was the one who pulled America out of the Great Depression.

Now FDR confronted an even greater challenge. The U.S. faced war on two fronts, in Europe and the Pacific. He famously called December 7th "the day that will live in infamy," and his speech is immortalized for lifting America's wounded morale in its darkest hour of need.

The sinking of the *USS Arizona*

But just three months later, FDR committed one of America's greatest tragedies. He signed into law the Executive Order 9066.

The Japanese Internment Act would be a regrettable stain on our nation's history.

Xavier: Why was the Act called that?

Hope: Unlike citizens of German or Italian heritage, Japanese Americans were considered "alien enemies." The federal government ordered us to close our businesses, leave our homes, and take only what we could carry. Any possessions we left behind were confiscated by strangers.

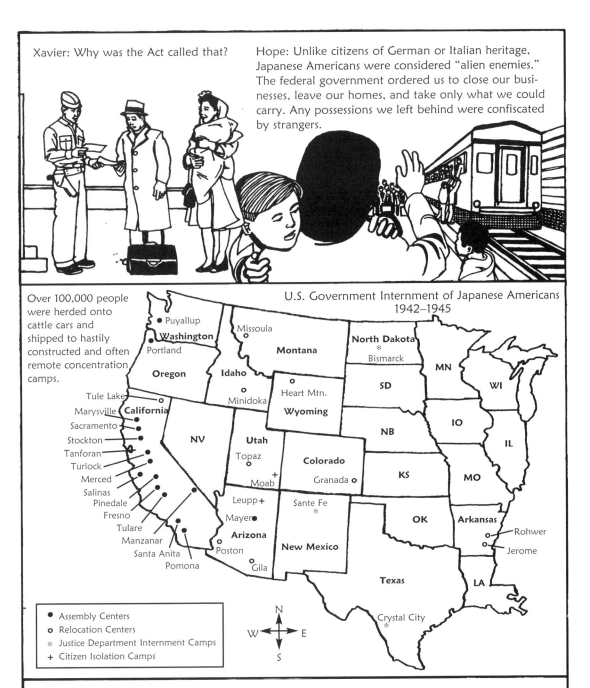

Over 100,000 people were herded onto cattle cars and shipped to hastily constructed and often remote concentration camps.

U.S. Government Internment of Japanese Americans
1942–1945

- Puyallup
- Washington
- Portland
- Oregon
- Missoula
- Montana
- Idaho
- Minidoka
- Heart Mtn.
- Wyoming
- North Dakota
  - * Bismarck
- MN
- SD
- WI
- Tule Lake
- Marysville
- California
- Sacramento
- Stockton
- Tanforan
- Turlock
- Merced
- Salinas
- Pinedale
- Fresno
- Tulare
- Manzanar
- Santa Anita
- Pomona
- NV
- Utah
- Topaz
- Moab +
- Leupp +
- Mayer
- Arizona
- Poston
- Gila
- New Mexico
- Colorado
- Granada
- Sante Fe *
- NB
- KS
- IO
- IL
- MO
- OK
- Arkansas
  - Rohwer
  - Jerome
- Texas
- LA
- Crystal City *

● Assembly Centers
○ Relocation Centers
✳ Justice Department Internment Camps
+ Citizen Isolation Camps

N
W ← → E
S

No charges, trials, or convictions were ever brought against us. We had no legal representation. We could not seek justice in a court of law. We were assumed to be guilty with no chance to prove our innocence. We were assumed to be traitors only because of our ethnicity, names, and color of our skin. Meanwhile, those in the Imperial Japanese armed forces were demonized as barbaric, inhuman monsters. So how could we Japanese Americans be considered anything less?

Xavier: What was life like in the internment camps? How did you meet your husband?

Hope: Frank and I had gone to school together. He was three years older than me but we were good pals. Coincidentally both our families were sent to Topaz, Utah. In the middle of dirty barracks, we had a bittersweet reunion. Of course there was no privacy to speak of.

TOPAZ ★WAR★ RELOCATION CENTER

During the day, it was dry, dusty, and hot.

At camp, no one had any fresh fruit or private provisions to eat.

Mothers, most of all, hated how everyone was forced to dine in the mess hall and stomach the cardboard meat, overcooked vegetables, and flavorless gruel. Not knowing how long we'd be there, some tried to grow their own food.

At night, the cold wind cut through the cabin walls.

On rare occasions, we might be allowed visitors.

My husband told me how one white friend of his family cried seeing them behind barbed wire. As a treat, she brought him and his older sister one precious apple each. Frank savored every bite, because it tasted like heaven.

Xavier: Wasn't there any way out of there?

Hope: We were stripped of all legal rights, even though we were American citizens. We didn't know how long the war would last. We didn't know how long we'd have to stay stranded in the desert, trapped like animals in a pen.

The only way out was to join the army. This was hotly debated in camp. Was this the best thing to do? We mulled it over for some time. Frank decided to enlist.

It was a strange time. Many friends had family in Japan who were fighting for the Emperor. Now they had nephews, cousins, and uncles fighting with other Asian Americans for the U.S.A.

Over 12,000 Nisei (second-generation Americans) answered the call. Many were segregated into the 100th Battalion/442nd Regimental Combat Team. Their motto was "Go for Broke," to accomplish the mission at all costs.

It was ironic. To prove our loyalty, our sons and brothers and friends and fathers had to be willing to sacrifice their very lives.

In France, to rescue the "Lost Battalion" of 200 Texans from being captured by the Germans, the 442nd suffered over 800 casualties.

100th   442nd

The 442nd became the most highly decorated unit in U.S. armed forces' history. They were fighting and dying to free people half a world away, as their own families were imprisoned at home.

[Xavier: The 442nd earned over 9,000 Purple Hearts and 5,000 Bronze Stars. In 2000, President Clinton awarded 19 men their long-delayed Medal of Honor.]

For all their heroism, they could only watch how President Harry Truman decided to end the war.

After FDR's death, Truman had to decide how he could eventually defeat Japan.

An American invasion of the islands was bound to be a grueling and costly affair, since the Japanese had proven to be tenacious fighters.

[Xavier: Truman chose the fastest, most lethal, and historically unprecedented option. On August 6, 1945, the nuclear bomb named "Little Boy" fell on the city of Hiroshima.

There the radiation will linger for thousands of years.

[Xavier: After being sued, in 1990 the U.S. government finally apologized for its errors and paid reparations of $20,000 each to the 60,000 internment survivors.]

On August 9th, "Fat Man" hit Nagasaki. From both attacks more than 100,000 Japanese citizens were killed instantly, with an equal number to die later from their wounds.

Japan capitulated a few days later and World War II was over.]

To this date, the U.S. is the only country ever in all of history to have used weapons of mass destruction.

Twice in four days, America intentionally bombed civilian targets.

When Frank came back home, he was a different person. Less carefree. More serious.

Then he attended college at the University of California-Berkeley on the G.I. Bill and studied economics. But in his heart he longed for peace and quiet. So he decided to be a gardener. He said plants don't talk back. He wanted to make things grow.

Frank and I were proud of raising our family and we enjoyed our retirement. He died just a year ago. In the past decade, more World War II veterans have been dying each day due to old age than the number killed in combat. Time, as always, proves to be the ultimate enemy.

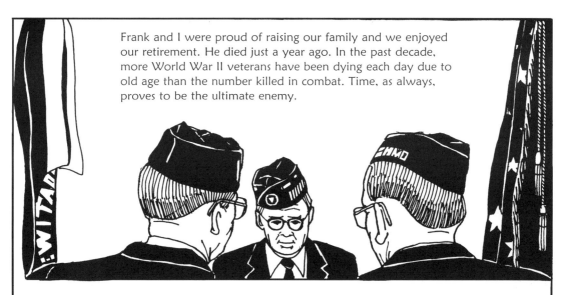

But if my husband were still alive, he wouldn't be happy with what has taken place. I'm sure Frank would have joined his fellow veterans and others who are standing up for the Arab Americans who have become victims of misplaced racism and discrimination. After what we experienced, we can't let it happen again.

Just like in the past, many people simply want to take action — to lash out against convenient targets without thinking or remorse. But scapegoating isn't the solution. Neither are secret tribunals. Ultimately people are better served by sound judgment, instead of hasty deeds that result in foolish regrets.

Justice often takes as much patience as persistence.

The crane is a symbol of peace.

Xavier: Through his wife's memories, Frank Nakamoto taught me again that wisdom and a steady hand can produce a beautiful and lasting legacy.

This word is pronounced "hei wa." It combines the Japanese characters of "Hei" (even) and "Wa" (harmony, gentleness, and peace).

"Wa" has profound social and philosophical meaning for the Japanese. Sometimes waging peace is much more difficult than war itself. I learned that from Frank. He told me so.

11th Grade History — Mr. Pearson: Class Report
Name: Julie Lai
Born: San Francisco, California, 1985

My family has been in America for four generations. My great-grandparents came from the southern Chinese province of Guangzhou, which Americans called Canton. At that time, getting into the U.S. from China was extremely difficult. Even today there are stories of Chinese who suffocate in shipping containers or drown at sea to get to America. Back then, thousands came searching for a better life. But the U.S. Congress passed the 1882 Chinese Exclusion Act. This was the first time that America had banned anyone from entering the country solely on the basis of their race. The act officially banned all Chinese immigration for the next decade, and it was renewed in 1902. The only way you could enter was if you were married to or an offspring of a person who was already here.

For some Chinese, their only hope was to change their last names on documents and claim fake parents. Those who succeeded were called "paper sons" or "paper daughters." Angel Island opened in 1910 as a processing center for immigrants, and one of my great-grandmothers was stopped there. Unlike on Ellis Island in New York, here people had to be interrogated about the legitimacy of their claims. For the unlucky who failed, Angel Island became a penitentiary.

The suspects were detained and quarantined within tantalizing eyesight of America. They called this promised land "the gold mountain," teeming with bountiful riches and boundless opportunity. Some who faced deportation chose to commit suicide, since they would lose face if they came back to China empty-handed. In 1940 Angel Island finally was closed, condemned by a fire. Three years later the Exclusion Act was repealed, as America sought China as an ally in World War II. Finally in 1965, President Lyndon B. Johnson rescinded these discriminatory racial quotas by passing the Immigration and Naturalization Act of 1965.

The Bay Area definitely has more cultural diversity than other places, and I grew up

I've enjoyed playing the piano since I was eight.

with friends from all over. But strangers still compliment me on my English and ask me what country I'm from. When I say I was born in San Francisco, they are surprised because they don't assume Asians are Americans.

When my mother was in college, she went to visit her roommate's family in Wisconsin for Thanksgiving. There she met someone who had never seen an Asian in person. This lady had to touch her skin to make sure my mom wasn't wearing make-up. I'm sure there are still places like that, where people only see Asian faces on TV.

However, I feel fortunate that my forefathers wanted to come to America. My grandfather reminds me how much things have changed for the better. My dad is a doctor in Berkeley, and my mom is a lawyer in Pleasanton. My older sister Samantha wants to go to dental school. My family has always prioritized getting a good education, but even we have a lot more advantages than my parents did.

I heard about Iman Farhi through my piano teacher. On Thursdays, my mother drops me off at Mrs. Walker's apartment to take my lessons, and Iman lives in the same complex. At first glance, we had nothing in common. But once she heard about my report, Mrs. Walker encouraged me to ask him for help. In turns out that Mr. Farhi is a pianist as well, and that they often talk about music.

Now that I've gotten to know Iman a little better, I don't think he's that much different from my family. Like my ancestors, he has endured a lot of hardship for the chance to have a better life.

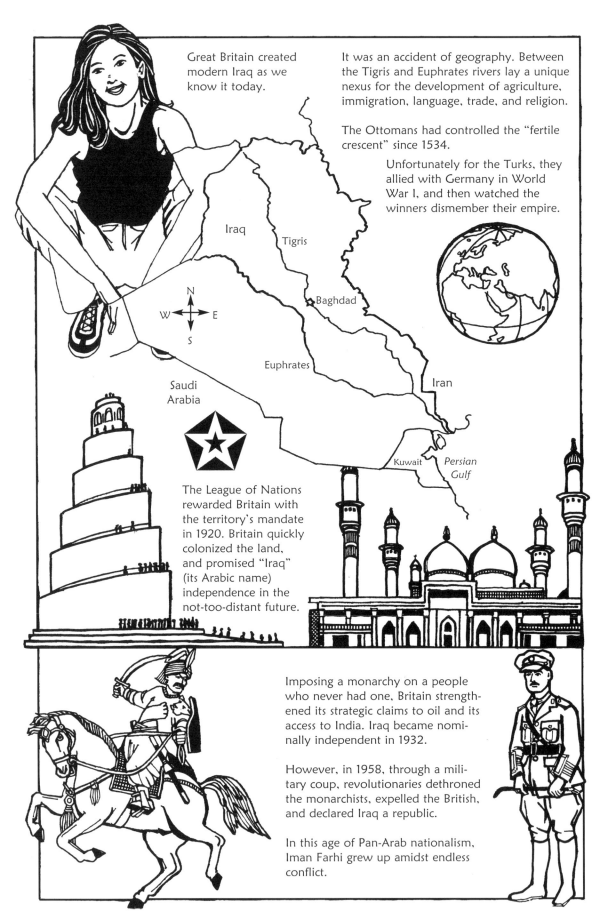

Great Britain created modern Iraq as we know it today.

It was an accident of geography. Between the Tigris and Euphrates rivers lay a unique nexus for the development of agriculture, immigration, language, trade, and religion.

The Ottomans had controlled the "fertile crescent" since 1534.

Unfortunately for the Turks, they allied with Germany in World War I, and then watched the winners dismember their empire.

Iraq

Tigris

Baghdad

Euphrates

Iran

Saudi Arabia

Kuwait

Persian Gulf

The League of Nations rewarded Britain with the territory's mandate in 1920. Britain quickly colonized the land, and promised "Iraq" (its Arabic name) independence in the not-too-distant future.

Imposing a monarchy on a people who never had one, Britain strengthened its strategic claims to oil and its access to India. Iraq became nominally independent in 1932.

However, in 1958, through a military coup, revolutionaries dethroned the monarchists, expelled the British, and declared Iraq a republic.

In this age of Pan-Arab nationalism, Iman Farhi grew up amidst endless conflict.

Julie: Why did you decide to leave your homeland?

Iman: I came to seek political asylum. I fled intolerance and bloodshed. I wanted to have freedom of movement, thought, and expression.

Now after what has happened in America since 9/11, sometimes I feel like I never left Iraq at all. Or that maybe I will even be forced to go back.

In this climate, the Federal Bureau of Investigation spies on any and all Muslim groups. They are all suspects.

The Immigration and Naturalization Service considers anti-American criticism to be signs of potential terrorism.

Students are trailed by secret police. Travelers are strip-searched. Anyone can be arrested without being charged. You can be interrogated without having a lawyer. You can be thrown into solitary confinement. Back home, the repression of human rights is well documented. To be treated the same way here is worse than fiction.

In 1979, Saddam Hussein became Iraq's president, after helping the Ba'ath ("revival") Party seize power in 1963. The first thing he did was wage war on Iran.

The U.S. sided with Saddam.

An Iraqi dissident, the Ayatollah Khomeini had overthrown Iran's Shah and held American hostages at the U.S. embassy in Tehran.

Let me remind you of some things that Americans may have forgotten. They did not happen that long ago, but then you were just a child.

[Julie: Committed to overthrowing the communist Sandinista regime in his own backyard, Reagan was frustrated with Congress for banning any aid to them.

Lt. Colonel Oliver North

Since this embarrassment toppled his predecessor, President Ronald Reagan vowed he'd never negotiate with terrorists. Yet he did. In 1986 the Reagan administration admitted to selling weapons to Iran to fund Nicaraguan "contra" rebels with the profits.

Also, Americans continued to be kidnapped, this time by Iranian sympathizers in Lebanon. To kill two birds with one stone, the CIA traded Iran arms in exchange for their influence in releasing American hostages, while funneling the proceeds to Central American militia.]

To save face from this scandal, the U.S. changed its foreign policy again to back Iraq. Buoyed with support from both superpowers, Saddam built a million-man army, rivaling even Israel's in armament.

Julie: Did the war improve things?

Iman: No. My generation has known nothing but misery. Iraq's war of attrition with Iran lasted eight years and ended in a stalemate. In the end it claimed a million casualties altogether. Baghdad is full of shrines to these fallen martyrs.

Iraq's war machine was financed by Kuwait and Saudi Arabia as well. However, after the war, Saddam was incensed that his Arab neighbors would not forgive his debts to them. Harboring this grudge, in 1991 he invaded Kuwait in retaliation. President George Bush led a coalition of nations, approved by the UN, to punish Iraq.

General Norman Schwarzkopf directed the allied forces in "Desert Storm." First they took back Kuwait and then conducted a massive aerial bombardment of Iraqi installations to weaken their defense. Then the U.S. poured countless tanks and troops across the Kuwaiti border and gave chase to Iraq's vaunted Republican Guard, who were now retreating across the desert.

The night sky of Baghdad was lit up with the glare of anti-aircraft fire and explosions from endless sorties. Screams of all sorts filled the city.

The memories still burn. To me, the funeral processions of 9/11 resembled the infamous Iraqi highway of death.

Desert Storm ended but Saddam still clung to power. His gambit to become the new Arab leader had failed, but he still held complete dominion over his ravaged nation. The foes he did not kill were imprisoned. I, for one, decided that if I wanted to survive I had to leave.

In 1990 the UN Security Council imposed economic sanctions on Iraq, to be lifted only when inspectors proved that all "weapons of mass destruction" have been eliminated.

Julie: Was this policy successful?

Iman: Only in further ruining a nation. Witnessing the damage caused by a total blockade, the UN soon permitted Iraq to sell $4 billion of oil a year to buy food and medicine. Later this limit doubled. But handicapped by oil price fluctuations and its devastated manufacturing capacity, Iraq still cannot maximize its "oil-for-food" quota.

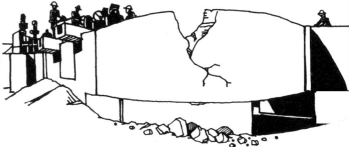

Julie: Do you mean peace was worse than war?

Iman: Allied bombing from Desert Storm destroyed most of Iraq's electrical grid, and water and sewage treatment plants. Most of this infrastructure still lies in disrepair.

However, sanctions have disrupted the whole economy and strangled supplies of food and medicine.

The UN claims to support child welfare. But in the 1990s, Iraq's child mortality doubled to over 10%. How can they allow more than 400,000 children to die from this policy? [Julie: That total is almost 2% of Iraq's total population.] Society has been decimated by malnutrition, the lack of power, the breakdown of health and sanitation services, and the spread of contagious diseases. Employment conditions have become sweatshops. Prostitution, child labor, and panhandling became rampant.
Innocent civilians became the victims.

[Julie: The oil-for-food program provides only $180 per person annually. That's 50 cents a day to live on.]

In the wake of 9/11, George Bush's son declared a "war on terrorism."

Now he has opened the door to the unknown: a never-ending, pre-emptive, and unilateral war.

I am part of Iraq's brain drain. Over two million educated professionals have left, many repatriating to England. But we still care and worry.

General Colin Powell was the heralded Chairman of the Joint Chiefs of Staff who led the U.S. forces to victory in Desert Storm. Now as Secretary of State he finds himself facing the past again,

SEC POWELL

Is it ironic that his voice is considered to be too moderate in this new war?

Meanwhile the Shiite majority watches and waits.

They don't forget that the elder Bush encouraged them to overthrow a weakened Saddam in 1991. However, when they rebelled, the U.S. called off its forces. Then the U.S. watched on the sidelines as the Iraqi rebels were brutally crushed by Saddam's reconstituted Republican Guard.

Would the outcome of another war be different?

In 1933, during the darkest days of the Great Depression, FDR motivated a shaken American public by proclaiming, "There is nothing to fear but fear itself."

Now have Americans become more afraid ...

than those that America claims it will liberate?

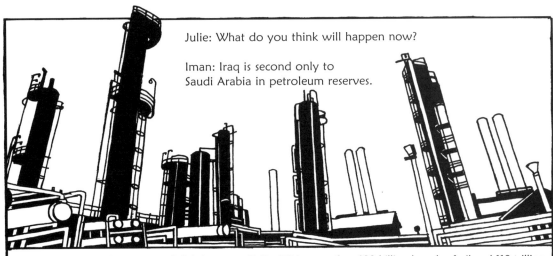

Julie: What do you think will happen now?

Iman: Iraq is second only to Saudi Arabia in petroleum reserves.

In an oil-crazy world, that is worth fighting over. [Julie: With more than 100 billion barrels of oil and 110 trillion cubic feet of natural gas, Iraq still is the U.S.' sixth-largest oil supplier and provides 8% of U.S. oil imports.]

King Fahd

What happened here in America was a tragedy. But why is the U.S. choosing to perpetuate another humanitarian crisis of far greater proportions?

Why isn't America doing something about Saudi Arabia, where 16 of the 19 hijackers came from? Or what about North Korea, which is resuming the manufacturing of nuclear weapons? Why is there such a double standard?

Kim Jong Il

To this day, the UN continues to deduct 30% of Iraq's oil sales for war reparations — claims for damages that total $290 billion. After knowing what happened to Weimar Germany under similar circumstances after World War I, how can they justify this? Many in the West have imagined how this burdensome isolation would succeed only in driving the next generation to become more extremist in the future.

In Iraq, I was branded a left-wing troublemaker. Here I am labeled a Muslim fundamentalist.

I empathize with Americans who have lost loved ones. But do they know of our pain? I shed no tears for Saddam. But thousands of people don't deserve to suffer even more because of the crimes of one man.

How hard is it to do the right thing?

11th Grade History — Mr. Pearson: Class Report
Name: Raman Patel
Born: Bangalore, India, 1985

It's not a coincidence that I come from a region that is known as India's Silicon Valley. There my father was educated as a software engineer and my mother was a science professor at a local university. After my youngest sister was born, they both believed that it was the right time to come to America. So when I was seven, my family decided to move here, to the real Silicon Valley.

When they first arrived, my parents had to make a lot of adjustments and even swallow their pride. Even though the standard of living is a lot higher in America, our family actually was less well off than we had been in India. In general India is incredibly crowded and extremely poor. My friends don't believe the stories I tell them about the living conditions there. But in Bangalore, my parents were prominent members of a respected family. We had inherited a large house, our own rooms, and servants like a cook and maid. We went to private school and our future there was fairly assured.

Now in America, it was all different. Suddenly we were anonymous foreigners with a handful of family or friends. The five of us lived in a two-bedroom apartment, and my two sisters and I had to share a room. We went to public school and were treated as outsiders.

Classmates said real Indians wore headdresses, threw tomahawks, and rode horses. The closest thing they knew about where we came from was *Jungle Book* and Mowgli. Better yet, they had not read Rudyard Kipling but had watched the animation. I told them that India was where Columbus wanted to end up. But he never made it there, and in 1492 he misnamed a continent full of natives. Throughout history, people have a way of perpetuating mistakes, well-intentioned or not.

Just to make ends meet, my parents took jobs far below what they were used to, both

The ritual of henna hands for an Indian bride.

in responsibility and salary. My father started as an entry-level computer technician. My mother stayed at home to take care of us and later found a job as a teacher's assistant. But they slowly worked their way back up the ladder. I appreciate their sacrifices to help secure our future. Now when my Asian friends tease me and call me "Noodle," I feel totally accepted...like I've really made it.

For my community service, I have been volunteering at a local senior citizens center for the past year. I have done a variety of things, such as organizing games, reading to them, or simply making conversation. Older people still have a lot to offer but tend to get overlooked here. Even though they may be retired and their bodies have slowed down, the elderly still have active minds. Maybe the world is just going too fast to pay proper attention.

There I saw Mrs. Kingfisher. The center's volunteer coordinator suggested that I introduce myself to her. In class, when we skip through periods and places, I find it hard to believe that an individual's life can be summarized in a few paragraphs. Mrs. Kingfisher proved to me that knowledge passed down among people carries a different but equally significant meaning. In the end, both of us looked forward to sharing her memories and wisdom. It was ironic that through an American Indian, I did learn more about myself.

Raman Patel: The Karuk Indians inhabit 1.4 million acres surrounding the Klamath and Salmon Rivers, in what is now Siskiyou County. One hundred people keep alive their endangered tongue. I spoke to one of them. Mrs. Kingfisher still had a lot to say.

Mrs. Kingfisher: I'm familiar with how, in the blink of an eye, a society can be shaken. Our tribe had lived here for ages, but life changed forever just 150 years ago.

[Raman: The U.S./Mexican War began on April 25, 1846, and ended two years later with the Treaty of Guadalupe Hidalgo. Driven by "Manifest Destiny," America annexed Texas and paid the conquered Mexicans $15 million for both New Mexico and California, destined to become the richest state in the richest nation on Earth.

Even before then, the U.S. was well aware of its wealth. In his departing speech to Congress on December 5, 1848, President James Polk displayed fourteen pounds of California gold. He promised that the government was "deeply interested in the speedy development of the country's wealth and resources." A year later Polk was dead. But in 1851 the California gold rush was on.]

History celebrates the rugged 49ers who sought their fortune. But to us they quickly brought ruin. [Raman: To clear room for more miners, the newly christened thirty-first state spent $1 million a year from its mining revenues to sponsor the murder of local Indians.

Official bounties to "Indian hunters" ranged from $0.25 for a scalp to $5 for a severed head. Entire villages were leveled in the process. In the Golden State, the native population fell by 90% during the 19th century.]

Raman: What problems did 9/11 reveal to you?
Mrs. Kingfisher: We've come a long way since the Plains Indians counted coop against their enemies. Before the age of guns, a Sioux warrior's greatest feat was to touch the forehead of his Crow foe in battle, not to take his life.

1776
Minuteman

1976
Minuteman
Missile

But that ideal of a warrior is out of date in today's society. Does it require skill or honor to push a button from a bunker or a plane to destroy families miles away? The character of warfare itself has become warped. When war becomes driven not by necessity but by expediency, we must re-examine what we are doing and why.

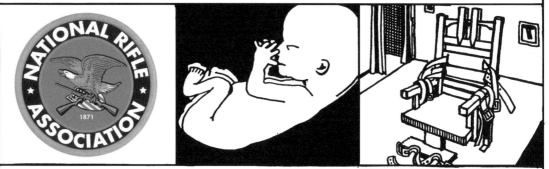

The hijackers weren't the first or only ones to turn America's own permissiveness against itself. So many freedoms are taken for granted. But then some are championed at others' expense. When people worship one right too much, they lose sight of how their community becomes fractured by such obsessive self-interest.

LINE
STARTS
HERE

When our consumer-oriented society can no longer provide instant gratification, it loses its guiding principles.

We are stuck in a time when the many must suffer greater inconveniences to prevent the potential transgressions of an unknown few.

When everyone is suspect, no one is free anymore.

Mutual trust becomes a relic of a simpler past.

Raman: What kind of wake-up call was 9/11 to America and the world?

Mrs. Kingfisher: It is one of many, with undoubtedly more to come. The world is out of balance, out of harmony with nature. Our tribal elders shared their wisdom and experience with us. They taught us to develop a viewpoint both practical and holy.

In this way, a simple salamander is seen as a good omen.

[Raman: The Pacific giant salamander is like a canary in a coal mine, whose presence signifies water purity. The Gold Rush could be better called the Dirt Dump. Twelve billion tons of land choked California's rivers. The Panama Canal's excavation was eight times smaller. Today water runoff is still polluted by mercury and other toxic metals.]

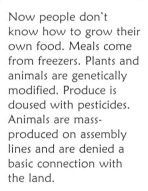

To maintain our rituals and lifestyle, we had to cooperate with our brethren. To ensure the survival of the salmon and ourselves, we collaborated with tribes from the Pacific Ocean to Oregon to allow the fish to swim to their spawning ground untouched. There was no mail. No phone. At the year's first ceremony of the fall salmon run, the Medicine Man was the first to partake of the fish.

Now people don't know how to grow their own food. Meals come from freezers. Plants and animals are genetically modified. Produce is doused with pesticides. Animals are mass-produced on assembly lines and are denied a basic connection with the land.

Upon contact with the white man, Indians also quickly lost their way, victims of alcoholism, disease, and suicide.

To survive, ironically we have preyed upon their weaknesses as well.

Now reservations make a killing selling cigarettes and running casinos. We have gotten revenge by becoming rich off exploiting the white man ... just like they have done to the Indians.

Raman: What is the Karuk view of life?

Mrs. Kingfisher: In Karuk mythology, the Coyote was involved in Creation. For other tribes, the Spider had a central role in The Great Mystery. Each is a trickster who symbolizes the paradoxes of life, death, and chance, all things creatures cannot control.

Linking stories of creation with ceremonies of renewal, people accepted their responsibility to nature. Animals were like people. They were spiritual beings. Nature was not separated into church and state. Since everything is connected to the land, the land is sacred and cannot be misused by special interests or selfish desires.

The Karuk tradition is to strap children into cradle baskets from birth. Immobilized for long stretches before learning to walk, a child is forced to observe. These childhood experiences shape adult attitudes: an individual is not the center of the universe but cared for as part of a larger ecosystem of relationships. By watching nature work at its own pace, we are not driven to dominate it.

Raman: How can our society be healed?

Mrs. Kingfisher: I don't have a prescription. I do know that a forest's health cannot be separated from that of the trees, or the owls, or the rivers.

Men log and pollute, valuing only short-term gain. But that damage, like cutting off a person's limb, will endanger the whole organism in the long run. People must see themselves as part of a larger system at work.

To improve one nation's health at the expense of another is both selfish and narrow-minded. The goal is to live in self-sustaining harmony. The path may be long and sometimes treacherous ...

but we must
walk it all the same.

Let me tell you a story. It is called "The Fire Race." In the beginning, the world was frozen.

Yet the three Yellow Jacket sisters were lucky because they alone had fire.

However, they refused to share it with other creatures ...

leaving them to shiver in the cold darkness. Some animals huddled together for warmth, and others dug burrows in the ground.

But the crafty Coyote hatched a plan. Soon he gathered all the animals around him and shared his idea with them.

The next night by himself, he quietly approached the sisters' fire.

Distracting them for a brief moment with his howl, the Coyote leapt over them. Grabbing a burning stick in his jaws, he sped away as quickly as he could. The Yellow Jackets buzzed in anger and joined in fast pursuit.

As they nearly caught him ...

the Coyote passed the stick off to the Golden Eagle.

Surprised, the sisters gave chase again.

But then the Eagle passed it to the Mountain Lion.

Then the Lion gave it to the Rabbit.

Next the Rattlesnake.

Then the Black Bear.

Then the Brown Squirrel.

Finally fire landed in the possession of the Frog. As they closed in, the Yellow Jacket sisters thought the chase finally was at an end.

The Frog wondered how he could escape. Desperate, he put a piece of burning coal in his mouth and jumped in the river. Frustrated, the three sisters had no choice but to fly back home.

When the Yellow Jackets had left at last, the Frog could come up for air. His mouth was burning! With a big relief, the Frog spit out a glowing ember on the riverbank. But suddenly the hot coal was swallowed up by the nearby Willow Tree.

Now why would the Willow want that piece of charcoal?

No one knew.

The tree didn't utter a sound, but just let its branches sway gently in the breeze.

Soon all the animals assembled round the tree. They wondered if their effort had been in vain.

Finally along loped the Coyote. With a twinkle in his eyes, he broke off two branches from the Willow, which made the tree weep ever so slightly.

Over a pile of dry moss, the Coyote rubbed the wooden sticks together furiously.

Now every time when our elders, or even you and your friends, gather around a fire to tell stories,

Soon sparks flew, the moss ignited, and fire was reborn for all to see.

animals too circle close to listen. That is how fire came to be, and the world was frozen no longer.

Raman: How do you make sense of the time we live in?

Mrs. Kingfisher: Unfortunately, today's conflicts are nothing new. Ohiyesa, also known as Charles Eastman, was a pioneering Indian writer. Born as a nomadic Santee Sioux in 1858, he graduated from Dartmouth College and chronicled his vanishing heritage. His poignant reflections, *From the Deep Woods to Civilization*, are as relevant now as when he wrote them in 1916, on the eve of World War I:

"Why do we find so much evil and wickedness practiced by the nations composed of professedly 'religious' individuals? The pages of history are full of licensed murder and the plundering of weaker and less developed peoples, and obviously the world today has not outgrown this system. Behind the material and intellectual splendor of our civilization, primitive savagery and cruelty and lust hold sway, undiminished, and as it seems, unheeded. When I let go of my simple, instinctive nature religion, I hoped to gain something far loftier as well as more satisfying to the reason. Alas! It is also more confusing and contradictory. The higher and spiritual life, though first in theory, is clearly secondary, if not entirely neglected, in actual practice. When I reduce civilization to its lowest terms, it becomes a system of life based upon trade. The dollar is the measure of value, and might still spells right; otherwise, why war?

Yet even in deep jungles God's own sunlight penetrates, and I stand before my own people still as an advocate of civilization. Why? First, because there is no chance for our former simple life anymore; and second, because I realize that the white man's religion is not responsible for his mistakes. There is every evidence that God has given him all the light necessary by which to live in peace and good-will with his brother; and we know that many brilliant civilizations have collapsed in physical and moral decadence. It is for us to avoid their fate if we can.

I am an Indian; and while I have learned much from civilization, for which I am grateful, I have never lost my Indian sense of right and justice. I am for development and progress along social and spiritual lines, rather than those of commerce, nationalism, or material efficiency.

Nevertheless, so long as I live, I am an American."

𝕖pilogue

> "See the world as your self.
> Have faith in the way things are.
> Love the world as your self;
> then you can care for all things."
> — Lao Tzu, *Tao Te Ching*, Chapter 13

Mr. Pearson watched the progress and reports of his class with a shifting mixture of trepidation and admiration. In the beginning, he was apprehensive that his students would succumb to laziness, apathy, or worse, boredom. But in the end, he was proud that they could become engaged, encouraged, and enlivened beyond their own expectations or his. They proved they could open their eyes to respect unfamiliar people, lives, and opinions. Indeed that boded well.

Despite the reluctance of some or the wishes of others, time does march on. Since Mr. Pearson's assignment, his juniors have become seniors. By the time you read this, most will have applied to college and graduated from James Madison High. Some friends decided to stay close to home, whereas others embarked upon journeys far away. They all "officially" are becoming adults and starting to make choices that will influence the rest of their lives and the world around them.

But the world they face is as challenging and confusing as ever.

From one defining moment, a series of events has unfolded that no one could have predicted, though many have become parties to the action. The world has continued to watch it all transpire from different angles. Barely a decade has passed since the first war that the elder President Bush waged against Iraq. The issues, stakes, and decisions seem the same ... but very different.

The arguments have raged within foreign embassies and across America's main streets. Who is detecting the sponsorship of terrorism or the development of nuclear arms? Enforcing or defying the mandate of the United Nations? Honoring the will of the people or the agenda of politicians? Promoting democracy or preserving dictatorship? Pursuing national self-interest or international consensus?

At the height of its military powers, displaying technological, logistical, and tactical superiority, the U.S. (supported by Britain) fought its way to the heart of Baghdad. In two weeks, their armies toppled a tyrant feared for over twenty years.

But in the process, the blood of countless soldiers and civilians has been shed. The true toll may never be known. Along the way, the U.S. has sown the seeds of discord among its staunchest allies and distrust among Middle Eastern and Muslim states. After receiving a nearly universal outpouring of sympathy a few years ago, ironically now the U.S. faces the greatest questioning of its global political legitimacy. Chaos has torn a nation and the new world order asunder. Who will reap this uncertain harvest?

In light of current events, citizens everywhere are still trying to make sense of 9/11. In the face of such adversity, the next generation can help point a way for a land of a thousand voices to find common ground. Our future may well depend upon it.

Reading Questions

Interview 1

1. What was your initial reaction to the events on September 11, 2001?

2. What is the proper global role of United States? Is it to be:
  a. the world's policeman
  b. the sole superpower
  c. the proponent of democracy or capitalism
  d. the protector of its own national interests

3. How should the U.S. combat terrorism?

Interview 2

1. What do you know about Islam?

2. Should the United States have attacked the Taliban in Afghanistan?

3. Do you consider yourself religious?

Interview 3

1. Why has the relationship between Israelis and Palestinians deteriorated over the past few years?

2. What should America's role be in mediating this conflict?

3. How can the Israeli/Palestinian problem be solved?

Interview 4

1. How has the discovery, development, and dependence on oil influenced America, the Mideast, and the world over the past century?

2. Why would some Muslims support or others oppose Al Qaeda's actions?

3. Are the goals of democracy and capitalism the same?

Interview 5

1. Would you serve in the armed forces or fight in a war?

2. Have your parents or someone you know served as soldiers?

3. How do you feel about the U.S. military recruiting on high school campuses?

Interview 6

1. What are the parallels between the American war in Vietnam and the Soviet war in Afghanistan?

2. What does the Vietnam Memorial symbolize?

3. What is the U.S. currently doing in Afghanistan?

Interview 7
1. Should Japanese Americans have been interned in World War II?

On a radio talk show on February 5, 2003, Congressional Representative Howard Coble (Republican, North Carolina) replied to a caller who suggested that Arabs in the United States should be rounded up and interned. Coble agreed that the internment of Japanese Americans during World War II was correct since "Some [Japanese Americans] probably were intent on doing harm to us, just as some of these Arab Americans are probably intent on doing harm to us." He praised President Franklin D. Roosevelt for establishing internment camps and claimed that they actually protected Japanese Americans. Coble stated, "We were at war. They were an endangered species. For many of these Japanese Americans, it wasn't safe for them to be on the street."

Coble is Chair of the Congress' Subcommittee on Crime, Terrorism and Homeland Security. In 1988 he made similar comments when he voted against paying reparations and extending a national apology to Japanese Americans who were interned during World War II.

2. Have American attitudes on accepting a multi-racial society changed in the past 50 years?

3. Should only some countries have nuclear bombs?

Interview 8
1. What do you remember about America's 1991 war in Iraq?

2. What do you know about the 2002 Patriot Act?

3. Did you support America's 2003 war in Iraq?

Interview 9
1. Do you consider yourself an environmentalist?

2. What is the moral of the fable "The Fire Race"?

3. Why are Charles Eastman's comments still relevant to Americans and current international events?

Conclusion
1. What questions would you have asked each of the people whom these nine students from James Madison High School interviewed?

2. How would you seek someone to interview in your own community?

3. How can you get involved politically and express your opinions locally or nationally?

4. How important are America's foreign and domestic policies to you, and why do they change from presidential administration to administration?

5. How can you hold your media, appointed officials, and elected representatives accountable for their opinions, decisions, and actions?

Recommended Reading

A Hope in the Unseen: An American Odyssey from the Inner City to the Ivy League, Ron Suskind, Broadway Books, 1998.

Afghanistan: A Russian Soldier's Story, Vladislav Tamarov, Ten Speed Press, 2001.

Black Hawk Down, Mark Bowden, Atlantic Monthly Press, 1999.

Cadillac Desert: The American West and Its Disappearing Water, Marc Reisner, Penguin, 1993.

Chink! The Ethnic Prejudice in America Series, ed. Cheng-Tsu Wu, World Publishing Company, 1972.

The Culture of Contentment, John Kenneth Galbraith, Houghton Mifflin, 1992.

Fax from Sarajevo: A Story of Survival, Joe Kubert, Dark Horse Comics, June 1996.

Firehouse, David Halberstam, Hyperion, 2002.

In Search of the Warrior Spirit: Teaching Awareness Disciplines to the Green Berets, Richard Strozzi-Heckler, North Atlantic Books; 3rd edition, 2002.

Light on the Indian World: The Essential Writings of Charles Eastman (Ohiyesa), ed. Michael O. Fitzgerald, World Wisdom, 2002.

Lincoln at Gettysburg: the Words that Remade America, Garry Wills, Simon and Schuster, 1992.

The Ox-Bow Incident, Walter Van Tilburg Clark, Vintage, 1940.

Our Stolen Future, Theo Colborn, Dianne Dumanoski, John Peterson Myers, Plume, 1997.

Palestine, Joe Sacco, Fantagraphics, 2002.

The Prize: The Epic Quest for Oil, Money, and Power, Daniel Yergin, Touchstone, 1991.

State of the World 2003: A Worldwatch Institute Report on Progress Toward a Sustainable Society, Ed. Worldwatch Institute, W.W. Norton and Company, 2003.

To Afghanistan and Back: A Graphic Travelogue, Ted Rall, NBM Publishing, 2001.

The Toughest Indian in the World, Sherman Alexie, Atlantic Monthly Press, 2000.

West of Kabul, East of New York: An Afghan American Story, Tamim Ansary, Farrar Straus & Giroux, 2002.

Where Do We Go From Here: Chaos or Community? Martin Luther King, Jr., Beacon Press, 1968.

Years of Infamy: The Untold Story of America's Concentration Camps, Michi Nishiura Weglyn, University of Washington Press, 1996.

Oliver Chin has dedicated his career to publishing and media communications. Graduating *magna cum laude* from Harvard University with a degree in Social Studies, he concentrated in Popular Culture and Mass Media. Formerly the editorial cartoonist for *The Harvard Crimson*, he has drawn for numerous publications such as Simon and Schuster, *Asian Week*, *Consumer Action*, *Street Sheet*, *New Mission News*, and the *San Francisco Call*. Called a "comics expert" by the *San Jose Mercury News*, he helped bring Japanese comics and animation into the American mainstream, and is a columnist for *Comics and Games Retailer* and *Comics Buyer's Guide*. Currently he resides with his wife and son in San Francisco, California.